BEYOND
PIPE DREAMS
— AND —
PLATITUDES

*Insights on Love,
Luck, and
Narcissism
from a
Longtime
Psychologist*

Geraldine K. Piorkowski, Ph.D.

outskirts
press

Use Your QR App
To Learn More Today

Acknowledgments

I WILL ALWAYS be grateful to the scores of psychotherapy/ counseling clients who openly shared their life stories with me and in the process taught me a great deal about human nature and the struggles of people to live meaningful lives with courage and compassion. Many thanks are also due to Debbie Carvalko, my former editor, for her helpful, editing assistance with this book. I will also be eternally grateful for the loving arms of my family: Frank, my loyal, supportive husband of sixty-one years; my two surviving children, Paul and Julie, for their ongoing affection and compassion; my deceased son Michael, who was forever hopeful; my daughter-in-law Jodi for her many efforts on behalf of the family; and my five grandchildren, Jon, Erik, Anika, Hugh, and Lia, for teaching me the value of play and laughter. And finally, I am grateful to the Creator for the many gifts so generously bestowed upon me.

Table of Contents

Introduction

WHEN I RETIRED as a clinical psychologist after more than fifty years of practice, I wondered: "What have I learned from all those varied experiences?" I had worked with people of various ages, races, cultures, sexual orientations, socioeconomic levels, professions, and geographical locations. In the mix of clients over the years was a nine-year-old pickpocket with a wide, girlish grin that lit up her face; a slew of lawyers, a number of whom were suicidal; a circuit court judge with family problems; a few physicians trying to resolve their romantic lives; a beautiful, light-skinned African-American model who was rejected by her family for not having dark-enough skin; a fifteen-year-old boy who accidentally shot and killed his brother; alcoholics of all kinds; and a politician running for statewide office whose wife accused him of domestic abuse. While such differences in descriptive trappings may seem profound, the communalities are what stand out for me.

Among the settings I worked in were mental health clinics, psychiatric hospitals, a home for delinquent girls, medical schools, private practice, and universities. In these diverse places I performed many functions, such as teaching, writing, administering tests, directing programs, supervising students, and counseling individuals as well as couples. I worked on the East Coast and the Midwest; in small towns, medium-sized ones, and big cities; in small clinics as well as giant hospitals that stretched over many miles. In all these varied worlds, no matter the differences in local culture, skin color, tattoos, or garments, people were more alike than different.

Besides the obvious physical similarities, psychologically people have the same needs, fears, defensive strategies, hopes, and dreams. While each of us has a different viewing lens for perceiving the world, a lens shaped by unique biological, familial, and cultural factors, we are fundamentally the same. We all want to be loved, appreciated, and understood. We want to matter to our friends and family and be special in some way to all those with whom we come in contact. We want to be self-sufficient and competent. We want space and time to be autonomous in pursuit of our dreams. We want to belong to a group, neighborhood, church/synagogue/mosque, or community—a place of welcome and acknowledgment. All of us want to feel safe in the neighborhoods where we live and be reasonably stress free. We also want some challenge in our lives, some novelty to reduce the boredom of ordinary days. And we want to feel good about ourselves; we want to walk around with our heads held high and a liveliness in our steps.

People everywhere are afraid of the same kinds of things. We are afraid of being assaulted, either physically or verbally. Because both physical and psychological dangers are threatening, one to our lives and the other to our identity, both kinds of peril create fear, tension, and anxiety. Contrary to the old children's rhyme we used to chant, "Sticks and stones may break my bones, but names will never hurt me," names, especially insulting ones, often hurt a lot. Betrayal, bullying, criticism, humiliation, manipulation, and rejection, all of which bruise our fragile sense of self, also hurt a great deal.

We are also afraid of having our inadequacies and our failings brought to light. When we are teased, taunted, or made fun of, our imperfections are made visible for all the world to see. We feel exposed as inadequate in some way and feel very vulnerable; we are not as strong, smart or "in control" as we would like. Because vulnerability is scary and psychological assaults hurt, people develop fears about these threats and build self-protective mechanisms to feel safe.

Trying to be safe, we may hide in our rooms or in our heads; lie to ourselves or others; counterattack the assaulters or carbon copies of them in person, by mail, e-mail, or social media; keep others at a distance by obnoxious behavior; or pretend we are very talented, wise, good-looking, or famous. The hiding can be literal, as when a teenager spends all his free time in his room, or symbolic, as when a doctor, lawyer, or engineer keeps her personal self out of sight and remains ensconced in her professional role. Rather than acknowledge hopes, dreams, failings, and inadequacies to close friends and family, professional recluses rely primarily on work-related skills to navigate erratically the world of intimacy and relationships. In this manner, they hide from their vulnerability in an attempt to feel safe and in control.

Hiding in our heads is a way of viewing the world from a vantage point above the fray. We can think all kinds of negative thoughts there, and nobody is the wiser. In this aerie in our heads, we are safe from counterattacks and free to be ourselves. Intellectuals, writers, academicians, and other creative souls are often in this group, because thinking feels a lot safer to them than feeling. Emotions are often intense, chaotic, and unpredictable, whereas thoughts tend to be logical and manageable.

Other ways of hiding include addiction to computer games. There, ensconced in technology, we avoid the unpredictable world of people by focusing on dragon slaying and war games. In that way we maintain a pseudo-connection to others with computer identities that do not risk much vulnerability and yet, satisfy our desires to be winning and in control. Addictions of all kinds are reliable hiding places that often last until physical dysfunction appears on the scene.

Other protection strategies include power-hungry maneuvers such as boasting, bellicose rants, and dictatorial strategies. Braggarts fill the conversational air with their accomplishments in hope that no one will notice how empty they feel. Similarly, bullies and dictators try to convince their worlds that they are powerful, when underneath it all they often feel helpless and insignificant. Angry, belligerent people who are adept at keeping people away are more comfortable with solitude, because closeness to others is fraught with emotional danger. Being betrayed, criticized, disappointed, insulted, and/or rejected are just a few of the perils they try to avoid.

While all the preceding observations have been underscored many times in my clinical and personal worlds, several new insights have emerged from my experience, some of which are counterintuitive, and others run counter to the prevailing culture in the United States. A new insight gleaned from my years of clinical practice contradicts the American culture's focus on the power of positive thinking. In contrast to this popular notion, I think it is safe to say that positive thinking is not always helpful. Platitudes (trite remarks used too often to be interesting or thoughtful) and happy talk do not prepare us for disasters lying just ahead. Every cloud does not have a silver lining, nor is there a pot of gold at the end of every rainbow.

Because the world is filled with all sorts of unhappy events, from disappointments and failures to losses, thinking only positive thoughts is delusional. Trying to maintain a happy face while tragedy engulfs us is unnatural, akin to trying to laugh when our hearts are breaking. Like Pagliacci, the clown who was intent upon making others laugh while tears streamed down his cheeks, we shortchange ourselves when we fail to deal with negative events and emotions.

Whenever there is heartbreak, no matter where it is coming from, the best way of getting through it is by acknowledging the sadness, disappointment, humiliation, or anger and then working through it. In a healthy person, the processing of negative feelings goes through phases, much like the waves of emotion that accompany grief, until we arrive at a personal resolution that uniquely fits us. The problem arises when people get stuck in negativity and can't move beyond it. In chapter one, titled "Positive Thinking Isn't All It's Cracked Up to Be," the limitations of positive thinking will be examined.

Another example, which was conveyed dramatically in a few words by a patient, jarred me when I first heard it. After weeks of catatonic behavior (severe motoric immobility that appears robotic and trance-like) followed by a psychiatric hospitalization, an African American man, who was forty years old, intoned, "Madness is better than sadness" as his first words upon recovering. When he was asked what he meant, he responded, "When you're mad you can do something, but when you're sad you can't do anything at all."

At this time in our culture when violence permeates the American scene in so many ways—there is video violence, domestic violence, street violence, school violence, and workplace violence—it is difficult to see how madness can be better than sadness. However, what the patient was communicating clearly is that anger is energizing and leads to action, while sadness is immobilizing and induces helplessness. Most of us would prefer to feel alive, in charge of our lives, and full of options, rather than depleted, stuck, and without possibilities. In chapter two, titled "When Is Madness Better Than Sadness?" the differences between daily, run-of-the-mill anger, narcissistic rage, and chronic anger will be explored.

Another cultural misdirection is our culture's obsession with romantic love. By way of scores of dating sites flourishing on the Internet, we run blindly toward the Promised Land of Eternal Love. We buy romantic novels, read manuals devoted to orgasmic ecstasy, and watch sophomoric movies filled with hormone-saturated teenagers groping their way to fulfillment. And yet, all this cultural energy devoted to love's arousal and maintenance doesn't alter the reality that romantic love (sexual feelings and emotional closeness) is basically an illusion. Because it is fueled primarily by fantasy, novelty, and emotional arousal, romantic love is almost impossible to sustain. Unless it is replaced by a quieter respect, admiration, or affection or contains some of those ingredients to start with, romantic love quickly dies and fades away in the light of reality. Chapter three, titled "Romantic Love Is Mostly an Illusion," will look at the fragility of romantic love.

Another idea that has emerged for me over the years is that vulnerable people are easier to relate to than assertive, self-confident ones. Vulnerability is an openness about feelings, successes, failures, strengths, and inadequacies as well as hopes and dreams. While our society imbues self-confidence with high status and desirability, and it is clearly invaluable as a personality factor, vulnerability is more appealing and more likely to foster intimacy. Vulnerable people are more readily trusted, nonthreatening, and likeable, whereas super-confident individuals earn our respect and admiration. We look up to confident people (they are our role models), but we are less likely to regard them as our best friends. Chapter four, titled "Vulnerable People Are More Likable Than Super-Confident Ones," will focus on the reasons why we are so conflicted about vulnerability, even though it is an appealing personality stance.

Other new understandings gained over the years that will be covered in subsequent chapters include the following:

Chapter Five: You Can't Make Anybody Do Anything. While punishment and torture work to some degree, they tend to create long-term resentment. In addition, all of us possess a degree of autonomy that cannot be manipulated under any circumstance.

Chapter Six: Luck or Chance Has Been Badly Underrated. Most of life (one's family, schoolmates, friends, teachers, roommates, romantic partners, and job prospects) is a function of timing and chance. Talent and hard work play significant roles in our achievements, but luck or chance is at least as important, if not more so at times.

Chapter Seven: A Smidgen of Narcissism Adds Joy and Spice to Life. Healthy narcissism embellishes personal achievements with delight and enhances lovability with charm. It provides the *joie de vivre*—the joy of living—that adds just the right amount of zest to ordinary life.

Chapter Eight: Empathy and Healthy Religion Go Hand in Hand. Empathy enables us to relate to others with care and compassion, while religion at its best provides a unifying, other-centered philosophy of life that reinforces our place in the universe alongside, not in opposition to, other people.

CHAPTER 1

Positive Thinking Isn't All It's Cracked Up to Be

WE LOVE POSITIVE people. The optimists are among our most admired, cherished friends. Seeing the world half full of joys and pleasures and not half full of disappointments is a blessed personality trait that makes it easier to get up in the mornings. As for the people at the opposite end of the continuum—the whiny, complaining ones, we avoid them whenever we can.

One of my all-time favorite humorous stories is about identical twins, one of whom was an optimist and the other a pessimist. Psychologists studied them to determine whether optimism and pessimism are influenced by the environment in any way. As part of their experiment, the psychologists put the pessimistic twin in a room full of toys and the optimist in a room full of horse manure. After an hour, one of the psychologists opened the door to the room with the pessimistic twin and found him crying in a corner. When asked why, he said he was crying because he was thinking of all the poor children in the world who had nothing to play with. When they opened the door to the optimist's room, they found him whistling and burrowing through the manure. When he was asked why he was so happy, he said, "With all this horse manure, there must be a pony in here somewhere."

For parents, other relatives, and teachers, the optimistic twin would be a delight to be around, while the pessimistic one would require lots of tending. In addition, children prefer being around their optimistic peers, who are popular and well-liked. Being able to see the positives in any dark, dismal situation is clearly an asset for individuals and those around them. If it rains on a carefully planned picnic or parade, for example, the person who has an alternate plan can save the day. Optimism is correlated with creativity, popularity, and self-esteem, among other factors.

LIFE IS NOT A BOWL OF CHERRIES

What is wrong with all this optimism and positivity? Nothing at first glance, except for the fact that optimism and positive thinking do not deal with all aspects of reality, and not dealing with reality can have negative consequences. Life is neither "a bowl of cherries" nor an endless stream of sunny days and happy moments. Reality has a dark side that needs to be confronted when we suffer pain, rejection, disappointment, loss, disease, death, and/or catastrophe, and for these things, happy talk, whistling in the dark, or putting on a happy face do not work. They interfere with problem-solving and action.

While optimism and positive thinking are correlated, they are different. Optimism can be defined as the tendency to put a positive spin on people and events; that is, anticipating and/ or seeing the world through a good pair of rose-colored glasses. Believing that things will eventually turn out all right—that there are silver linings to most clouds—is a wise and healthy perspective. However, when we believe that only positive thoughts are worth having and that negative ones will lead to depression, we are caught in an untenable, self-limiting bind. Like a politician painting a rosy, unrealistic picture of the future and a salesman hustling to make a sale, we are deluding ourselves and others.

SUZY SUNSHINE AND HILARIOUS HARRY

The perpetually smiling individual who is super-saturated in positives is great for laughs but hard to be around when disappointments strike. Typically filled with platitudes, the super-happy person relies on stock phrases to offer encouragement in times of stress. "Don't worry; there are lots of jobs out there" is meant to cheer up the recently fired friend, but it typically falls on deaf ears, and the rosy job forecast may not be true. "He's in a better place" said to a grieving friend who just lost her husband can come across as hollow and insincere and often does little to comfort the friend. Unless the bereaved is a staunch believer in an afterlife and the departed husband was a saint, such platitudes can be discordant, jarring, and difficult to absorb. One woman who had just lost her daughter to suicide was so upset by her friend's thoughtless remark about the daughter being in a better place that she ended their relationship on the spot.

Because people who are always positive are basically inauthentic, they are hard to relate to. Their cheerfulness in the midst of our despair further compounds our unhappiness. Not only do we feel down and discouraged because of life's disappointments, but being around Miss Susy Sunshine results in further questioning of our self-esteem. Feeling misunderstood, we wonder why we can't be as resilient or as positive as our perennially cheerful friend or neighbor.

Men who have a need to be funny, the Humorous Harrys of our social world, try to cheer us up with wisecracks when we are feeling down. While their humor can bring a smile to downcast faces, Humorous Harrys are not easy to talk to about job problems, social rejections, or physical ailments. When the world is not funny, the court jesters' attempts to distract us fall flat. Their intentions are honorable but their antics questionable.

The super-positive people who read self-help books on improving relations with others learn that everyone loves a compliment. Armed with this insight, these individuals dispense compliments like candy wherever they go. While the compliments initially feel great, they tend to be indiscriminately dispensed and as a result are gradually distrusted. When a compliment is given for a dirty T-shirt or a messy hairdo, the compliment loses its veracity and credibility. And with the loss of credibility is a loss of trust in the honesty of the compliment giver. The need of super-positive people to be liked clouds their judgment and reduces the likelihood of their becoming lifelong friends or partners.

THE LIMITS OF POSITIVE THINKING

Life is full of daily doubts, disappointments, and minor mishaps. From the spilled cup of coffee to the twisted ankle, life offers a daily smorgasbord of pleasures and frustrations, some obviously more serious than others. The spilled cup of coffee or the missed bus on the way to work are frustrations worthy of an emphatic "darn" without further ado. The minor mishaps do not warrant further attention;

they are just an inconvenient part of life, akin to a rainy day spoiling our outdoor plans or a long-awaited, personal phone call coming through just as we're sitting down to a business meeting.

As for the more serious obstacles or tragedies, ignoring them or forcing positive thoughts does not erase the frustration, sadness, disappointment, fear, or anger. Because strong emotions have much energy accompanying them, the emotions need to be dissipated or worked through, or the emotion gets locked into habitual ways of thinking and being. When strong emotions occur, they prepare the body physiologically for vigorous action, and when action is not possible or desirable, strong emotions ordinarily fuel negative thoughts or they spill over into tears.

Working through feelings means experiencing the emotions, not wallowing in them, and letting all the accompanying thoughts pass through awareness until we arrive on the other side. In this manner, negative emotions lose some of their energy, and we become open to other, more positive viewpoints. Self-awareness followed by praying, crying, and/or talking to others is the best way of getting through difficult feelings and moving beyond them. Unless negative feelings are processed, that is, experienced, thought about, and resolved, they can create psychological symptoms, poor judgment, chronic irritability, and/or low frustration tolerance. Road rage, which is sweeping the highways of the United States, is one current example of misdirected anger that results from unprocessed feelings that belong elsewhere.

PSYCHOLOGICAL SYMPTOMS: THE PRODUCT OF UNRESOLVED FEELINGS

One young woman in her mid-twenties came into psychotherapy complaining of panic attacks that began shortly after a one-night stand ended badly. She was intoxicated at the time and her sexual partner, an admired acquaintance, left abruptly in the middle of the night without saying a word. While she had strong feelings about her partner and his rejection, she denied that his behavior meant anything to her. Every time she saw him at a bar with his friends, though, she had a full-blown panic attack, or at the very least, a milder episode of "nerves." Her tendency to deny stressful, negative feelings had a long history going back to her mother's death of cancer when she was ten years old and her father's remarriage to a cold, rejecting woman at the time the patient was in her early twenties. Psychotherapy was beneficial in helping her identify triggers and resolve her negative feelings.

Similarly, a young man in his mid-thirties had strong, negative feelings that he was unable to process at the time about his wife's alcoholism and her affair with a coworker. Later, however, when he was divorced and dating another woman he was strongly attracted to, he began to feel upset and distrustful about his new love for no apparent reason. Only after he began counseling sessions and acknowledged the pain of being betrayed by his former wife did his anxiety symptoms and distrust of his new love abate. Currently he is happily married to his second wife with an "and they lived happily ever after" ending.

In another situation, an elderly woman in her eighties could not tolerate negative events and feelings. Often commenting that talking about such events left her depressed, she would change the topic to a happier one whenever a negative subject, such as pain or mortality, came up in conversations. Her inability to tolerate the dark side of life left her agoraphobic (highly fearful of crowded streets and other public places) and quite depressed on occasion, even when there were no apparent causes. In addition, her Pollyanna attitude interfered with her judgment, resulting in her making poor decisions about important life events, such as the ongoing care of her mentally impaired son. She could not acknowledge the negative aspects of his condition, and as a result failed to get him the kind of medical care he needed. Her difficulty in dealing with that tragedy inadvertently led to his untimely death.

GRIEF: A NORMAL TIME FOR NEGATIVE THOUGHTS

With profound grief, which is often experienced after the death of an important parent, sibling, child, or romantic partner, it takes at least six weeks at minimum, and more typically a year, before there is an enduring resolution. Even after that, memories will be triggered throughout life by reminders of that person.

During the time we're in mourning, many different images, thoughts, and feelings, both positive and negative, about the deceased person will be experienced as we go through different stages of grief.[1] Whether we're in denial, anger, bargaining, or sadness about someone's death or our own potential demise, as when facing a serious upcoming surgery, the natural, psychological rhythm of loss keeps us moving from one feeling or stage to another. As our minds and bodies

---

1   Elizabeth Kubler-Ross, *On Death and Dying*, New York: Simon & Schuster/Collier Books, 1970.

start to heal, the character of our thoughts and feelings will gradually change, becoming more accepting over time. With a healthy or resilient person, there is no need to superimpose positive thinking on the process. It will occur naturally and be of our own making.

Trying to maintain a happy face while tragedy swirls around us requires super-human strength or an uncanny ability to maintain a public persona no matter what is going on personally. While such extraordinary effort is tiring, it also robs us of the needed personality resources to cope with the disaster. When all our psychic effort is geared toward pretense and not healing, we wind up in a shallow, superficial spot. We can talk "the power of positive thinking" but feel none of it. Walling off the negative feelings, we have less available energy to use healthy, adaptive coping strategies.

Clearly there are times, especially in our professional worlds, when the mask of sanity needs to prevail, no matter how heartbreaking our personal losses. When this occurs, it is important to be aware of the emotional turbulence beneath the surface and allow times at the end of the day for self-soothing and emotional expression.

UNRESOLVED GRIEF

Unresolved grief can take its toll by keeping us up at night. Insomnia, depression, and other psychological symptoms are often the residue of an aborted grief reaction. One college student came to the university counseling center complaining of intense panic reactions upon seeing middle-aged men of a certain body build on the street. The strangers resembled his father, who had died suddenly a year earlier. While the student said he felt nothing at the time of his father's death, it was shortly thereafter that his symptoms began.

Markedly ambivalent toward his father during his life, the college student became immobilized emotionally when his father died and was unable to sort through the myriad feelings his father's death unleashed. Ranging from relief to anger to sadness, his feelings were a complex mixture that was difficult for him to process. Eventually, through counseling, he was able to experience the feelings of grief he had buried, and along with this awareness the surge of anxiety toward paternal look-alikes disappeared.

Besides people whose significant relatives have died suddenly, recent amputees are another group with major difficulty working through grief. Whether the limb loss was necessitated by diabetes, circulatory problems, a war-time injury, or a vehicle accident, the amputation is often sudden and life-changing. Their lifestyle, athletic prowess, autonomy, and independence are all changed dramatically as a result of the amputation.

Fearing that negative emotions will be overwhelming and permanent, recent amputees, especially men, try hard to focus on their present-day challenges, such as learning how to maneuver with only one leg or walk with a prosthesis, rather than deal with grief. They do not want to succumb to "a pity party," which will further erode their self-worth, because most of them believe that men don't cry nor should they complain about life's injustices. In the face of tragedy, men are supposed to suck it up, at least that is what they have been told or led to believe.

Harry, a seventy-five-year-old amputee, talked positively during his first week of hospitalization about his amputation and the abundant family support he was receiving. But during the second week, he experienced an impulse to jump out the window, saying that the only thing that stopped him was his fear of heights. While the impulse to jump seemed to come "out of the blue," it was a residual of the unacknowledged grief and hopelessness he was experiencing at some level. Fortunately, compassionate staff members at the rehabilitation facility where he was an inpatient helped him come to terms with such moments of despair. While sadness and other negative feelings, such as anger, humiliation, and inadequacy, are common after a person experiences amputation, such feelings need to be worked through, or else they result in chronic depression.

DEPRESSION: AN OUTCOME OF UNRESOLVED GRIEF

The primary danger of not dealing with grief is the kind of severe debilitating depression that robs the joy out of everyday life. The severely depressed person has no energy to handle any of life's challenges, no curiosity about any new experience, and no interest in daily pleasures, including eating. Sleeping excessively throughout the day and looking forward only to the next pain pill often define the daily life of depressed people. Their difficulty in facing grief can be compounded by their relatives' inability to deal with negative emotions. As one recent amputee said, "No one wants to be around you when you're sad. They only love your chipper self."

Even well-meaning friends and relatives feel helpless when their grief-stricken friend is depressed, angry or guilt-ridden. Relieved when there is any sign that their old friend is back to "normal," friends and relatives often prematurely reinforce the fledgling moments of positivity and inadvertently block the grieving process.

For the grief-stricken person who is guilt-ridden, depression accompanied by suicidal thoughts and feelings can be a serious outcome. With guilt-laden depression, the grieving person feels responsible for the loss. In the case of amputation, for example, the amputee may believe that smoking caused the circulatory problem that triggered the amputation. Or if the amputation was the direct result of excessive alcohol or drug use, the amputee feels to blame for the chronic substance abuse. When the amputation was caused by diabetes, diabetics may feel guilty because they were not careful or consistent enough with dietary restrictions in their lives.

When there is grief related to the death of a significant person, guilt frequently occurs because of real or imagined actions that bereaved people believe contributed to the death. If only they had not been angry when they last saw the person or been kinder or visited more frequently, their friend or relative would still be alive. Very often these guilty deeds are minor transgressions in the eyes of the world, but to the guilt-prone, they are real sins of omission or commission. Regardless of how the behavior is judged by others, the depressed person feels guilty and worthless.

With guilty depression, suicide is a risk. Feeling that their mistakes are unforgiveable, depressed people, especially those who take on too much responsibility for life's accidents, tend to be self-blaming. In the face of catastrophes, they may see suicide as their only option. Whenever this happens, professional help, including medication, is needed because the suicidal person is stuck in a downward spiral of negative thinking and emotions.

LIFE'S ORDINARY TRAGEDIES

The heartbreaks of daily life—the unrequited love, the disappointing academic or sports performance, the failure to get a job promotion, the betrayal by a friend, and /or the sickness of a parent—strike regularly and often without much notice. They are part of human existence. There is no way around them; getting through them intact is what is important.

We have all been disappointed when we didn't get the academic grade we wanted, were turned down by the college we had dreamed about, were ignored by the attractive person sitting right next to us, or were passed over for the job we felt ideally suited for. While all these disappointments can be painful, they are equal opportunity destroyers of happiness. Without exception we are all victims of life's misfortunes at one time or another.

The best way of getting through ordinary tragedy is by processing the event; that is, acknowledging the sadness, disappointment, humiliation, or anger, and letting the corresponding thoughts work their way through our consciousness. As the negative emotions dissipate, we can then become open to other perspectives. For example, we may begin to see that we are not defined by our recent failures and that life tomorrow is full of other possibilities, no matter how difficult today's disappointment is.

Self-awareness of negative thoughts is often the jumping-off point for the development of a broader, richer worldview. And when this nuanced perspective is arrived at by the person himself, it is not a cliché but a deeply felt understanding that leads to resilience[2] in the face of tragedy. Resilience is that in-

---

2   E.E. Werner, *Vulnerable but Invincible: A Longitudinal Study of Resilient Children and Youth,* New York: McGraw-Hill, 1989.

effable quality that allows some people to come back at least as strong as before after being knocked down by life. Being able to bounce back after misfortune is a gift that resilient people appear to possess in abundance.

When the natural, healthy flow from negative feelings/thoughts to optimism about the future is bypassed in favor of platitudes, however, a superficial adaptation without much depth is likely to occur. Suzy Sunshine dancing through the tulips is unlikely to be an Oracle dispensing much wisdom. Repression of negative thoughts and feelings eliminates creativity, resiliency, and resourcefulness from its landscape in favor of superficiality.

For others trying to adopt a positive stance, the hackneyed platitudes may sound empty. The silver lining in every cloud and the pot of gold at the end of the rainbow appear too insubstantial to hang onto for any length of time. If the cliché is too flimsy to grasp, we are left empty-handed, trying alone to make sense out of an unbelievable loss or an unimaginable disappointment.

THE CHRONIC COMPLAINER

With pessimists who see disaster lurking behind every corner, their negative thinking is a way of life—a habitual means of viewing the world. For the Chicken Littles of the universe, every sunny day is viewed as a temporary respite from the dark gloominess of life. Seldom finding pleasure in a glorious sunset or a magnificent piece of art, they tend to judge most things as imperfect—as flawed fundamentally. Their unhappiness permeates most aspects of life, coloring their world a dark gray. Their negativity is chronic, almost ingrained, and palpable.

When we meet a chronic complainer on the street, we hesitate to ask our culture's most common question, "How are you?" We hesitate because of how predictably the complainer, without much regard for our time or interest, responds with a stream of maladies. We are thus conflicted about how to greet this person. When we finally inquire about the complainer's well-being, we are bombarded by a lengthy discourse, in which we learn more than we ever wanted to know, for example, about the intricacies of esoteric diseases. Every ailment the complainer is experiencing is given its due with much detail and flourish.

Chronic complainers adopted negativity long ago as part of their personalities. Their dark viewing lens was shaped by imitation of role models, many catastrophes, or a lifelong pattern of failing to deal with anger. In the first instance, parents and other caretakers were embittered by life's disappointments, passing on their cynicism and bitterness to their children. In many daily occurrences, these parents conveyed to their children a negative, hopeless perspective on life.

In other cases, complaining became habitual as a result of one disaster after another. For example, the father in a family may have lost his job, leaving the family struggling financially, while at the same time, the mother may have become ill and unable to care for the children. As a result of such extreme misfortune, the children would be highly stressed trying to handle neglected parental duties along with their own school responsibilities. Juggling cooking, household chores, and baby-sitting with schoolwork can create bitterness that finds its outlet in nonstop complaining.

In still other situations, chronic complaining and cynicism began as a response to repressed or suppressed anger. Unable to express anger directly in their families, these children spent their time daydreaming angry scenarios, participating in video war games, and/or reading crime stories. The parents in these families were often bitter themselves, but they refused to allow their children to show anger. Often constrained by childrearing and religious beliefs, these parents were unaware of the contradictions between their behavior and their expectations regarding their children's conduct. They punished their children for expressing anger while doing so with much anger. By behaving in this way, they modeled the very behavior that they were punishing.

IN SUMMARY

For chronic complainers and other chronically negative people, exercises in positive thinking are often useful. Focusing on the positives in their lives—the people and experiences that are beneficial—can be a way of changing the habitual course of their thinking. In addition, being grateful for life's blessings is a healthy pursuit for all of us that can create humility and goodness in the world.

However, positive thinking is not the cure-all for all of life's disasters. When positive thinking bypasses the processing of negative events, it can limit our thinking and stifle internal resources. Happy talk, for example, often short-circuits our ability to plan for disasters that are lying just ahead. In addition, not working through negative feelings can lead to anxiety, depression, other psychological symptoms, alienated relationships, and impaired judgment.

Poor judgment occurs when the negative aspects of a situation are ignored rather than addressed, for example, when a starstruck lover pays no attention to the repeated rebuffs by his beloved and continues to pursue her relentlessly, or a parent turns a blind eye on the excessive drinking and/or poor health of a family member rather than upset anyone. Denial of negative symptoms also leads people, especially men, to ignore bodily signs of illness, which results all too frequently in disability or early death.

Instead of excessive reliance on denial, realistic thinking, which includes self-awareness of negative feelings and thoughts as well as positive ones, is the healthiest perspective to adopt in the long run. Because realistic thinking acknowledges the depth of sadness that can accompany major losses and disappointments, it can facilitate the resolution of grief and other trauma-related emotions for those of us not permanently wearing either rose- or dark-colored glasses.

Realistic thinking can also provide a blueprint for change, whenever change is possible. Even with unchangeable events like death, realistic thinking is often the catalyst for the initiation of worthwhile activities, such as memorial funds, scholarships, or political movements. Many of the parents who lost their children in the Sandy Hook mass killings in 2012 in Newton, Connecticut, [3] for example, became anti-assault weapon activists and devoted their lives to this cause. Acknowledging and processing negative feelings—not walling them off—is the most reliable means of resolving them, which then allows us to move onto other, more positive perspectives and actions.

---

3   Peter Schworm and Melissa M. Werthmann, "Profiles of children killed at Sandy Hook Elementary School," *Boston Globe*, Dec. 18, 2012.

CHAPTER 2

When Is Madness Better Than Sadness?

THE PHRASE "MADNESS is better than sadness" was uttered by a catatonic patient in a psychiatric hospital upon his recovery. Three weeks earlier, the forty-year-old African American man named Harold had been in a catatonic state, where he was silent and immobilized for hours on end. At that time he stared straight ahead, not moving a muscle, as if frozen in a prehistoric Ice Age. When Harold was asked, "Why is madness better than sadness?" he answered, "When you're mad you can do something, but when you're sad, you can't do anything at all." By madness he was referring to anger, not insanity.

Harold was talking about the energizing effect of anger in contrast to the energy depletion that typically accompanies sadness. He was right. When we are angry, we are ready for action. We want to fight, throw something, or head for the hills at top speed. The energy pulsates through our being looking for some sort of outlet. Sadness, on the other hand, has the opposite effect. Sadness, the emotional state brought on by important losses or extreme disappointments, leaves us immobilized. It robs us of energy and leaves us staring out the window. Since nothing can be done to alter most sad situations, especially losses that are the result of death or permanent abandonment, there is no energy in pure sadness. We are left to cry silent tears, and we have no words.

TO BE OR NOT TO BE: THAT IS THE QUESTION

In Harold's case of catatonia, he was immobilized not only because of sadness but also because of conflict. His wife of many years had left him, and he was conflicted about her desertion. Vacillating between sadness and anger, he was unable to move. Just as Shakespeare's Hamlet was immobilized and indecisive after his father's murder and his mother's sudden marriage to his uncle, the murderer, so Harold was caught up in conflicted feelings. To be sad or angry is often the question!

Sensitive, intelligent, and thoughtful people are often conflicted about anger. Taught to be polite and compassionate toward others, they are anxious when angry. Not comfortable in expressing anger directly, they are more at home with sadness. Because sadness typically has no motivational charge, however, they feel hopeless about changing any aspect of the frustrating situation.

An example of the motivational impetus of anger versus sadness occurred in a workshop dealing with anger. In the workshop a forty-five-year-old, overweight, passive woman talked sadly about her unhappiness with her marriage. During one exercise that focused on her feelings about her husband, she got visibly angry and chased the stand-in for her husband out of the room. While the transformation from sadness to anger was dramatically evident in her red face and loud voice during the workshop, what was most surprising was her weight loss the following year. She lost a grand total of forty pounds that year and began a new job. Clearly she got in touch not only with anger, but also with the accompanying motivational energy she then used for highly constructive ends.

In a similar case, a professional woman—a lawyer—was overwhelmed by grief over the rejection by "the love of her life." At the same time he was seriously dating her, he had been secretly involved with another woman, whom he finally decided to marry. For months thereafter, the lawyer suffered a debilitating sadness over his betrayal until one day when she received a perfunctory apology from him in the mail. At that moment, she experienced a surge of such intense anger that she was finally able to let go of her attachment and move on. The old phrase "Hell hath no fury like a woman scorned" is not only valid, but fury can be highly productive, especially when it propels a person forward in a positive direction.

THE BENEFITS OF ANGER

Besides the energy and motivational boost that often accompany anger, expressing anger directly communicates information more intensely and more quickly than any other message.[4] When someone we know is angry, our ears perk up and we listen attentively. Anger amplifies the message; it turns up the volume of the communication. Anger is both riveting and powerful.

---

4   Charles Duhigg, "Why Are We So Angry?": The Untold Story of How We all got so Mad at One Another, "*The Atlantic,* Jan/Feb 2018, pg. 63-75.

In addition, as Olga Tokarczuk, a Nobel Prize winner for literature, wrote,[5] "Anger makes the mind clear and incisive, able to see more. It sweeps up the other emotions and takes control of the body. Without a doubt, anger is the seat of all wisdom. Anger has the power to exceed any limits." She also talks about how anger simplifies a complicated situation and makes obvious a given course of action.

However, because angry people are often dangerous, we try to ascertain how threatening a specific situation is before reacting when the anger is directed at us. Should we fight, flee, or try to maintain a rational discourse in the unpredictable moment? Regardless of what we decide, we are on red alert and intensely listening to every word of the message during the encounter.

If we are not a blamer, we, along with two-thirds of the recipients of anger, will come to realize our mistakes and try to make up for them. In most of the episodes studied where anger was expressed in a restrained manner (no screaming at the top of one's lungs, throwing things, or hitting),[6] the situations were much improved after the angry confrontation and not made worse in any way. In these research studies on anger, the overall ratio of beneficial to harmful consequences was three to one. In general, short restrained outbursts of anger tended to make bad situations much, much better.[7]

For the person expressing anger directly, there is a sense of relief—a feeling of authenticity. We feel true to ourselves,

---

5   Olga Tokarczuk, *Drive Your Plow Over the Bones of the Dead,* Fitzcarraldo Editions, London, England, 2009 p.27, Translation copyright by Antonia Lloyd-Jones, 2018.

6   James Averill, "Studies on Anger and Aggression: Implications for Theories of Emotion," *American Psychologist,*1983, 38, (11), 1145-1160.

7   Charles Duhigg, "Why Are We So Angry?" (see note 4).

genuine, integrated. Something important got said, and if no one was permanently hurt, there is nothing to worry about. Helplessness vanishes, and we are ready to move forward. We feel in control and in charge of life.

In addition, people who express anger in a restrained manner are perceived as competent, powerful, and strong. They are viewed as leaders who overcome obstacles and not passive victims willing to absorb whatever injustice gets thrown their way. They are activists and doers—people who are admired and respected.

WHERE DOES ANGER COME FROM?

Anger is the emotional result of the frustration of a need, desire, or expectation. Identified decades ago as the frustration-aggression hypothesis, the relationship between these two variables, frustration and aggression, is not as clear cut as we might assume. Sometimes when we are frustrated we may kick a can or the dog or scream at our neighbor. At other times, we may quietly bemoan our lot in life and drown our sorrows in a glass of beer or two. At still other times, we may channel the frustration into fury at the opposing team in baseball, football, or hockey.

What we do with the frustration is related to our upbringing, our culture, our values, and our personality, among other factors. In cultures and families where civility and courtesy reign supreme, any outward expression of frustration is frowned upon. Being deferential and gracious to another person is highly valued, whereas frankness and rudeness are abhorred. Traditionally, Asian countries were well-known for their polite demeanor and hospitality, but in more modern times, the assertiveness and brashness of the West have permeated their cultures, but fortunately, not to the same extent as in the West.

As for personality differences, introverts are more likely to internalize the frustration; that is, think about it for hours on end, and/or blame themselves for the incident. When bumped into, for example, introverts would be quick to say to the other person or to themselves, "I'm sorry. I should have watched where I was going." Introverts tend to be intropunitive; that is, self-blaming, rather than blaming of others.

In the same situation, an extravert, especially those who are also blamers, might say to the other person in an angry tone of voice, "Why don't you watch where you're going?" In general, blamers are quick to transfer responsibility for wrongdoing to others, and in the process absolve themselves of any guilt for mistakes that spring up around them.

EXPECTATIONS AND ENTITLEMENTS

When ordinary expectations are not met, we get disappointed. A friend not remembering our birthday or our boss not rewarding us with a well-deserved raise are disappointing experiences that ordinarily result in sadness, not rage. There are plenty of disappointments to process as we go through life—from the poor grade in school to the failed performance in sports or music to the rejection by the boy or girl of our dreams. Daily we encounter disappointments provided by the weather raining on our parade or insensitive friends pursuing their own ends and not ours.

But somewhere along the way, modern culture added a sense of entitlement to the mix of disappointment and sadness, which became transformed into rage. The sense of entitlement is a narcissistic belief that not only do we deserve special privileges, but we also have a right to them. It is the belief that we are entitled to whatever we want, whether front row seats, the best tables at restaurants, or the best treatment wherever we go. By virtue of name, title, position, or accomplishment, the world owes us something, and when this something doesn't occur, the narcissists among us are insulted.

ROAD RAGE, COMMON NARCISSISTIC INJURIES, AND REVENGE

The widespread phenomenon of road rage in American culture attests to the role of entitlement in creating anger. Why should anyone get angry about being caught up in a traffic jam or being cut off while transferring lanes? We may be in a hurry, want to get someplace quickly, and do not want to be treated rudely by anyone, including other drivers. Some frustration in these circumstances is understandable, but If we accepted the reality that we could be slowed down in busy traffic and that other drivers might be rude in difficult circumstances, we could adjust our expectations accordingly.

Instead we have come to expect that we should have smooth sailing the minute we set our automobiles on an interstate. When that expectation isn't met, we grow impatient and often enraged. Our hopes and desires for quick and easy travel have grown into entitlements. We now feel entitled to drive as fast as we would like and beware the driver who gets in our way. This sense of entitlement on our highways often leads to reckless driving and tragic accidents fueled by road rage.

For many drivers, highways are perceived as war zones filled with enemy combatants lurking behind every billboard. Any slow-moving driver getting in their way or aggressive driver making minor traffic infractions is viewed as a major impediment to their right to run roughshod over their territory. Such behavior clearly reflects a sense of entitlement.

Similarly, our impatience at long lines in grocery or department stores reflects an underlying expectation that we should be able to move through the world at our own pace. If we need to move rapidly, then the people around us should accommodate our desires. If we walk slowly, then the crowds behind us should walk around us, no matter the inconvenience to them. Our wishes and desires have become expectations, and our expectations have turned into narcissistic entitlements.

Not being addressed respectfully, for example, may be an affront to our dignity. Likewise, not being paid attention to socially when we expected otherwise is a slight. Whenever we were hoping to have a lively conversation with someone and instead were ignored, we are hurt. But being outraged at such experiences bespeaks another quality; namely, that of narcissistic entitlement. Royalty has a right to be offended when ignored, but we lesser mortals should settle for hurt and/or disappointment.

Revengeful people are another group of angry, entitled individuals. They often hang onto their anger for decades, intent on exacting revenge on those who have wronged them. While the occasions triggering revenge motivation can range from the most inconsequential, such as losing a game of cards, to the most devastating, such as being raped or attacked, the intensity of revenge fantasies does not depend on the seriousness of the incident, but rather on the personality of the one who was offended.

People intent upon revenge have inordinate difficulty in gaining perspective and letting go. "How *dare* they—" is a frequent thought that keeps their outrage going. Unfortunately, even when their wildest, revenge fantasies have been fulfilled, they find little satisfaction. In most instances, revenge itself does not bring closure or gratification.

MORAL OUTRAGE

Another kind of transformation of anger occurs with moral outrage. Moral outrage takes place when frustration and disappointment are joined by a deep-seated sense of injustice. In moral outrage, religion and ethical principles are typically involved. Rather than being narcissistically entitled, morally outraged persons see themselves as victims of a profound offense to their dignity as human beings. Cesar Chavez and his grape pickers, Martin Luther King and his marchers, and civil rights workers all over the world were angry because they were being treated in a manner not befitting their status as human beings.

Currently, members of the Me-Too movement in the USA are outraged that they have been treated as sexual objects, not as human beings. Members of the "Black Lives Matter" movement are angry because of racial inequality and injustice. Victims of police brutality or gun violence are angry because they were assaulted in a manner that undermines their dignity and endangers their lives. Union strikers and protestors of all kinds—for clean air or water, for better working conditions, against toxic waste, against fracking, and more—are voicing their outrage at unfair governmental or business practices that demean or endanger them. Whether their moral outrage will be channeled into productive activities, such as marches, sit-ins, or nonviolent demonstrations of some kind, will depend on the leadership, ethics, and tactics of any campaign or movement they join.

THE CHRONICALLY ANGRY

Besides narcissistic anger and moral outrage, chronic anger is another variant. The chronically angry person seems to be frustrated most of the time and ready to explode as if sitting on a powder keg. Anything and everything can set him off. Road rage is his frequent companion, along with many other grumblings and disenchantments. He is angry at the mayor of his town, the governor of his state, and the president or prime minister, all of whom he believes are doing a poor job. The managers of his favorite, but losing, sports teams, the landlord of his apartment building, and his boss at work are all frequent targets of his wrath. They are all viewed as hopelessly inept.

Underneath all that anger is a major disappointment or two—hurricane-like setbacks that have thrown him. He may have lost out on the promotion he was hoping for, his wife may have left him, and/or his children turned out poorly. He may have screwed up a major sales account or his friends may have turned on him. Whatever has befallen him got turned into rage that he regularly unleashes. Like Willy Loman in *Death of a Salesman*,[8] he is depressed and feels worthless but blames others rather than himself.

In addition, our modern-day Willy Loman often drinks too much. Rather than drowning his sorrows in beer, he finds that alcohol amplifies them. While the first two drinks will work their magic and relax him, the rest of his binge drinking that night will put him on a fast-moving train through emotional upheavals of all kind. After three or four drinks, he often will become indiscriminately angry at all the people who have actually or potentially injured him. And then after five or more drinks, self-pity and depression will take over. During this last

---

8   Arthur Miller, *Death of a Salesman* (New York: Penguin Books, 1996).

stage of a binge, he is frequently morose, tearful, and self-hating, literally crying into his beer. The following day, while hung over, he forgets how sad he was and is ready to be angry at the world again rather than at himself.

Most of the people who are chronically angry are blamers who have very low self-esteem. Not especially self-aware, they tend to act out their conflicts in angry outbursts rather than silently stew about their miseries. Frequently they are loners who are also paranoid to some degree. They see others as unsupportive, if not out to get them. Other people are tolerated, not trusted. They are unhappy with the world, but most of all they are unhappy with their lives, which they feel powerless to change. In situations where domestic violence occurs, blamers attack their partners, verbally and/or physically, because their fragile sense of masculinity is threatened and assaultive behavior enables them to feel powerful and in control.

Clearly, the chronically angry person affects everyone around him with his angry outbursts. The partners of chronically angry people are themselves at risk of becoming chronically angry through secondhand exposure. In the same way that secondhand smoke can cause cancer, so secondhand anger creates a toxic environment that is frustrating and harmful to the people around. Because his friends and family cannot understand why anyone should be so unhappy, they are hurt and baffled by the chronically angry person's behavior. In addition, if they are sensitive people, they are likely to blame themselves for some of the anger in the home atmosphere, which results in their own self-esteem suffering.

THE DANGEROUSLY ANGRY PERSON

What changes a chronically angry person into a dangerous one? People can simmer in their anger for most of their lives without physically hurting a soul. Alcoholics and drug addicts are often angry individuals who typically destroy themselves, not others. In contrast, a dangerously angry person is clearly a blamer who attributes his misfortunes to the misdeeds of either specific individuals or society at large, rather than himself. In addition, he does not have much of a sense of right and wrong. Antisocial or psychopathic personality disorder, which refers to a pervasive pattern of disregard for the rights of others, lack of remorse, deceitfulness, and impulsivity, is a common mental health diagnosis of those who are angry and dangerous.

Full-blown paranoid tendencies—that is, strong feelings of being persecuted by others—are also quite common. The paranoia could be focused on known individuals or on aliens from outer space. In the former case, the focus of the paranoia is on individuals who are believed to have been a source of abuse, such as bullies, bosses, or teachers. In the latter situation, schizophrenia—a severe, psychotic mental illness where the lines between reality and fantasy are blurred—is usually the basis of the paranoia.

While such predisposing personality factors are common, including social isolation and a desire for fame/notoriety, there is usually a precipitant—a recent event that puts the chronically angry person over the edge. The precipitant typically involves a dramatic loss of self-worth, as in a job firing or a betrayal from a romantic partner. When additional fuel is added to the emotional baggage of a chronically angry person, an explosion is likely to occur. Mitigating factors are family support, strong religious identification, and/or strong values against violence.

THE ROLE OF CULTURE IN ANGER

A scrutiny of a culture's art, drama, literature, movies, music, and TV will shed light on its demons. Since the beginning of the twenty-first century, Western culture has become replete with violent imagery and sounds. If aliens were to visit, they would be shocked at all the violence that permeates the American scene. There is domestic violence, school violence, gang violence, and workplace violence, among others.

Since the 1990s, the death toll from mass shootings has risen dramatically in the United States— from Columbine's highly publicized school massacre of thirteen individuals by two high school students in 1999 to the Las Vegas shooting in 2017, which resulted in fifty-eight deaths that included the gunman. Between 2011 and 2014, the rate of mass shootings in the United States has tripled, according to Wikipedia, 2020. Since then the numbers have escalated even further, with 434 mass shootings in 2019 that resulted in 517 deaths.[9]

Violence is dramatically evident in American motion pictures, where guns and assault weapons blazing away can be seen in almost every picture frame. While movie settings have changed during the last century, from cowboy prairies to war-time combat zones to gangster-infested city streets, and more recently to science fiction/horror arenas, violence is the common ingredient throughout these films. Enemies of all shapes and sizes are to be found everywhere, and survival in the face of imminent threat seems to be the major goal in life,

---

9   "Mass Shootings in the United States in 2019," *WIKIPEDIA*, April, 2020.

according to the American motion picture industry.

In the United States, popular TV comedies of the second half of the twentieth century that dealt with family conflicts, such as *I Love Lucy* (1951-57), *All in the Family* (1971-79), and *Everybody Loves Raymond* (1996-2005), have been replaced by drug and violence-filled series, such as *NCIS* (2003-present), *Breaking Bad* (2008-2013), and *Game of Thrones* (2011-2019).

While movies and TV shows may exaggerate the prevalence of violence, what is clear is that people throughout the world at the beginning of the twenty-first century *are* angry. They are angry because they are lonely and do not know how to get their basic need for human relatedness met in a society on cell phones and computers. They are angry because they are frustrated that they are not as valued or loved as they had desired. They are angry because there is massive wage and social inequality, and they are near the bottom of the totem pole. They are angry because everywhere they look, including computers, movies, and social media, they see people doing much better than they are. They are angry because the basic rules of civility—the "please" and "thank you" of yesteryear—have vanished, and everywhere they go, they are treated rudely. And they are angry because they are scared—afraid of foreigners, terrorists, rapists, and murderers—and being angry is a more powerful tool than fear.

Further adding to the accumulation of cultural anger is the prevalence of anger merchants who know how to profit from anger. Academic courses dealing with the use of anger in debt collection and negotiation are being taught in prestigious business schools, no less. There students are taught how to be manipulative in negotiations by intensifying anger to get what they want. In training programs in other settings, debt collectors are taught how to use anger strategically—when to fake it, when to cool it down, and when to be understanding, all in the service of collecting more money.[10]

At this point in history, the West is an angry place, and so is the East. In the West, politics revolve around fear and nationalism rather than globalism and cooperation, and in the East, around survival, territorial acquisition/maintenance, and national identity. Terrorists intent on revenge magnify anger, keeping it alive in an endless cycle of recrimination, rumination, and ever-expanding fury. "Blood never sleeps," a phrase that shows up in spy and terrorist novels, aptly conveys the never-ending cycle of violence that begets more and more violence. In such angry cultures, peace and prosperity have little room to exist, much less thrive.

PARENTING, ANGER, AND NARCISSISM IN CHILDREN

Just as cultural violence begets more violence, so do angry parents beget angry children. Children who are shouted at, beaten repeatedly, and treated inhumanly in other ways imitate their parents' behavior in their own dealings with others. Frustrated and angry by their parents' abuse, they copy their violent behavior because it appears to be a powerful and effective tool in getting what they want. The children of violence are the bullies of the world who perpetuate the cycle of violence in their own neighborhoods.

While the relationship between angry parents and angry children may be obvious, what is not clear is the relationship between parenting and excessive narcissism in children. What factors breed narcissism among today's children? Or

---

10   Charles Duhigg, "Why Are We So Angry?" (see note 4).

phrased another way, what accounts for the rapid growth of entitlement in modern culture that adds combustible fuel to normal anger?

Part of the growth in narcissistic entitlement is due to excessive focus on the self-esteem of children at the expense of concern for others. In modern countries we are too worried about hurting our children's feelings and not enough about how their behavior impacts others. We try too hard to convey to our children that they are right no matter what they do, that they can be anything they want (which is not true), and that the rights of others are of no consequence. We value assertive behavior in our children much more than kindness and quiet thoughtfulness. And when it comes to competition versus cooperation, competition clearly wins out. The competitive, outspoken child who pushes his way to fame and glory is viewed as the ideal youngster in the American culture of the twenty-first century.

In addition, we do not spend enough time teaching our children about life. We don't let them know regularly and emphatically that disappointments, hurts, and betrayals are as much a part of life as joys, delights, and pleasures; that others have rights just as we do; that we'll never get our own way all the time; that winning is less important than doing your best; that failure doesn't feel good, but it doesn't define us; and that honesty and integrity are the hallmarks of a good person.

IN SUMMARY

Much as we would like to eradicate anger from our world, it will always be with us, informing us about what is important in our lives. While the frustration of basic needs and desires will typically be met with some negative emotion, it does not have to be bitter, unbridled, and dangerous anger. When tempered with restraint, anger can change interpersonal dynamics. When coupled with justice, it can be a powerful voice for change. But when mixed with narcissistic entitlement, anger can be a destructive tool that perpetuates the endless cycle of violence that never sleeps.

When anger is expressed directly at the time it occurs, there is less likelihood of anger becoming chronic. With restrained expression, the chances of anger seething under the surface, gathering intensity until an explosion occurs, are lessened. And with modulated expression, there are more opportunities to be heard and the underlying issues resolved as a result.

Conversely, without some tempered expression of anger, the chances of anger being converted into sad, depressing feelings are increased. The psychoanalytic view of depression as anger turned inward has more than a grain of truth to it. To avoid full-blown depression, even a simple self-acknowledgment that one is angry lessens the kind of hopelessness that leads to passivity and despair. Being aware of our own anger is empowering in itself, for it provides the opportunity to decide how to handle the anger in a given circumstance.

If we teach our children and others that the frustration of their desires is disappointing and at times hurtful but that feelings are transitory, they will learn that they can survive negativity in life. This acceptance from parents and teachers alike and the resulting self-awareness will lessen the possibility of negative feelings being transformed into chronic anger or rage. Self-awareness of hurt feelings and disappointments reduces the sting and intensity of life's arrows, permitting us to savor life's pleasures, whenever they come our way.

CHAPTER 3

Romantic Love Is Mostly an Illusion

HOW SHOULD WE describe this thing called *love*? Fragile or powerful, eternal or fleeting, volatile or steady, safe or treacherous? Ephemeral and magical, love can be as hard to hang onto as a wisp of smoke or a cool summer breeze; yet it can be as strong and enduring as steel or granite. Love can sneak up on us, catching us by surprise, or develop slowly, like advancing age. Its sudden onslaught can be overwhelming or its slow, steady pace difficult to discern. Full of contradictions, love is impossible to pin down with any degree of certainty, and yet everyone would agree that love is a valued emotional state, worth devoting considerable time and energy to its pursuit and maintenance.

Romantic Love, nature's mating call, is a blend of sexual desire and emotional attraction that is difficult to define. Some writers try to distinguish romantic love from romantic passion by adding emotional intimacy (feelings of connection and caring) to the erotic pot,[11] but even with emotional closeness, ro-

---

11   Robert Sternberg, *The Triangle of Love,* New York: Basic Books, 1988.

mantic love frequently does not last. When a young man was asked on Valentine's Day what love is, he answered, "I think it's really just a feeling. When you're in love, you just kind of know. It's pretty indescribable." What he did not know was that feelings are not permanent fixtures; they come and go, changing over time.

Because romantic love is evoked to perpetuate the species, it has strong biological or unconscious underpinnings. In addition, fantasy, novelty, and emotional arousal[12] play dominant roles in determining its intensity as well as influencing partner choice. In contrast to filial love, friendship, patriotism, or parental love, romantic love is not especially loyal or trustworthy. It can vanish at a moment's notice without the cement provided by friendship, shared values, or a commitment, which is why today's version of romantic love does not have much staying power. As for sexual attraction without emotional appeal, it has an even shorter life.

Romantic love, without sustaining factors, is an illusion that is subject to the love-eradicating effects of ordinary routine. Especially in those countries that overvalue romantic love, like the United States, relationship satisfaction in romantic relationships drops significantly after the first year. And it continues to decrease unless something dramatically changes; that is, unless there is some realignment of the interpersonal dynamics in the couple. Otherwise, the relationship continues with both members unhappy or the relationship ends. The high divorce and separation rates for marriage and live-in partners throughout the world further attest to

---

12　Sharon S. Brehm, Rowland S. Miller, Daniel Perlman, and Susan M. Campbell, *Intimate Relationships* (3rd ed.), Boston: MA: McGraw Hill, 2002.

the fragility of romantic love. In addition, the decreasing cohabitation and marriage rates worldwide strongly support the proposition that romantic love is in trouble during the first part of the twenty-first century.[13]

FANTASY: THE PRIMARY APHRODISIAC

Fantasy, the primary driving force in romantic love, is seldom fully conscious. Operating below the level of rational thought, fantasy—a creation of our imaginations—colors our perceptions of a loved one, painting him or her with idyllic features. We project our desires onto ordinary souls. The blue-eyed, muscular truck driver becomes Hercules, and the curvaceous, petite blonde is transformed into a beauty queen as she captures our heart. Fantasy transforms ordinary people into super-special ones. Whitewashing flaws and magnifying positive qualities, our imaginations create the ideals that our hearts seek. With smoke in our eyes, we struggle to see clearly the hazy beloved image before our eyes.

The role of fantasy in determining love choice is apparent in most love selections, regardless of age, sex, education, race, culture, or geography. Examples abound in movies, TV shows, operas, songs, and ordinary life. For example, a highly revered, brilliant psychiatrist might appear at a professional gathering with his gaudily dressed wife, who looks more like a harlot than a life partner, and his colleagues are taken aback. "What in the world does he see in her?" reverberates throughout the hall. Similarly, when an attractive model walks into the theater with an wizened old man twenty-five years her senior, a comparable question circulates in the air about

---

13 Geraldine K. Piorkowski, *Adult Children of Divorce: Confused Love Seekers,* Westport, CT: Praeger, 2008.

her choice.

I vividly remember a client, an accountant, who repeatedly described his wife as among the most beautiful women he had ever met. One evening I met his wife, who was waiting for him in the lobby. Much to my surprise she was among the least physically attractive women I had ever encountered. In his loving eyes, however, she apparently was quite beautiful. The old saying "Beauty is in the eyes of the beholder" has great validity when it comes to love choices. This wise saying also warns us of the futility in trying to talk a friend or relative out of a poor love choice. "But he doesn't have a job" or "She is a gold-digger," or "He drinks too much" will fall on deaf ears. Our admonitions are likely to create resentment rather than acknowledgment because the bedazzled lover feels misunderstood when we do not share his perceptions. Not privy to his pipe dreams, we cannot appreciate the fantasy-enhanced view he has of his beloved.

When a loved one is criticized, the lover typically responds with a rationalization or two. The woman whose boyfriend doesn't have a job might say, "Even if he doesn't have a job, he is trying to find one, but nobody is hiring right now. And besides that, he is loving and kind." The fact that he has not had a job for months while others in his trade or profession have no difficulty in getting or keeping one is lost on her.

The man attracted to the gold-digger tells himself that her excessive spending and repeated pleas for money are reflections of her good taste and that she does love him for himself, contrary to all the evidence. The woman attracted once again to an alcoholic man tells herself, "He doesn't drink every day; he only drinks too much at social gatherings." This justification follows repeated criticisms from family and friends that the man of her dreams drinks like a fish and has done so for years.

Why is one woman attracted to blond, blue-eyed, intellectual types while her best friend is attracted to swarthy, muscular ones? Even in the same family, why is the sister's romantic attraction so different from that of her siblings'? The answers reside in the unique personal histories of each person—their relationships with caretakers, their unresolved conflicts, their values, their ideal self, and/or their interests. Through romantic attraction, people try to work out the missing, valued, or conflictual aspects of their personalities.

THE IMAGO: RADAR FOR MATE SELECTION

The imago, [14] the semiconscious compass on the lookout for familiar qualities and values, operates to ensure that we find people to gratify our needs, at least partially. The imago is a composite picture of the people who influenced us most strongly at an early age, whether mother, father, siblings, a babysitter, or a close relative. Unfortunately, the imago does not always have our best interests at heart when it goes about its job of finding familiar people for us. While we may be attracted to positive qualities that were especially meaningful to us, for example, our kindly grandmother's smile or our loving father's loquaciousness, others may be attracted to ambivalent qualities that were a source of conflict in their early years.

When the romantic attraction is based primarily on the positive qualities of a beloved caretaker or relative, the adult relationship stands a good chance of surviving. With appealing but ambivalent characteristics, the mastery motive, or the desire to overcome anxiety-laden experiences, often comes into play and sets the stage for intensely dramatic, romantic

---

14 Harville Hendrix, *Getting the Love You Want: A Guide for Couples,* New York: Henry Holt & Co., 1988.

liaisons. With primarily negative experiences during the formative years, adults frequently avoid romantic entanglements altogether or search for partners that have diametrically opposite traits; that is, characteristics markedly different from those of their caretakers.

The mastery motive, which is the human desire to gain mastery over anxiety-ridden or difficult experiences, operates in all of us and is dramatically evident in the toddler's repeated attempts to walk upright despite regular falls or the budding musician's endless rehearsals of the same song until it is perfect. In romantic love, mastery motivation is evident when a parental figure had both highly positive and negative characteristics (for example, a successful, widely admired father who was, however, rejecting and critical of his daughter). In such a scenario, what commonly occurs is that the adult woman finds herself attracted to professionally successful men who are also critical, but she is not aware initially of how critical they are. Mastery motivation, while blind to negative qualities, provides the impetus for love journeys filled with hope and determination.

When the honeymoon phase of such a relationship is over, however, the adult daughter often becomes disillusioned by her partner's lack of affection and questions why she ever got involved with him in the first place. While such an initial attraction does not make rational or conscious sense, underneath it all she was hoping to have a different sort of relationship, a loving and accepting one, with someone outwardly similar to her father. Because "hope springs eternal," she wanted to rewrite her new love story with a happy ending.

The mastery motive keeps us supplied with an endless stream of similar types. The woman who finds one alcoholic lover after another and the man who keeps choosing unfaithful women for life partners are trying to rewrite their personal histories and supply them with positive outcomes. Unfortunately, the mastery motive is not a particularly effective mechanism for providing what we really need, because it blindly seeks a reenactment of the past without regard for the totality of the person before us.

NEEDS FOR COMPLETION AND VALIDATION

Another motive that frequently leads us astray is the need for completion. Falling in love with people who possess qualities we admire but lack ourselves is another fantasy-laden motive that does not deliver. Typically, these qualities are ones we value highly and wish we had. In other words, they are part of our ideal self—the self we aspire to be. For example, a shy woman may fall in love with an outgoing man, a life-of-the-party type, with the hope that some of his gregariousness and spontaneity will rub off on her. When it doesn't happen, she is disappointed, and the quality she admired—his desire to be the center of attention with humor and wisecracks—will become a source of irritation to her.

Similarly, the boyish man who lacks discipline and hopes to be transformed by a super competent woman is bound to be frustrated when she nags him repeatedly to grow up. As a result, his admiration for her competence will quickly fade and he will become unhappy. As for his wife, Ms. Super-Achiever, she will soon be overwhelmed by all the chores that fall on her shoulders because of Peter Pan's neglect. While she may have been initially attracted to his boyish charm and hoped that she would incorporate some of his playfulness, his childish irresponsibility eventually becomes highly frustrating to her. The self-enhancement she had hoped for never takes place because she was too busy being a grown up.

Another example where the need for completion was only briefly fulfilled is Henry and Cynthia's relationship. Henry was a successful businessman who made millions in the stock market, but weighing in at 350 pounds, he was physically unattractive. Although highly intelligent and witty, he had not had any long-term relationships with women, ostensibly because of his weight, until he met Cynthia.

In contrast to Henry, beauty was Cynthia's strong suit. While she was a very attractive model, Cynthia lacked financial security because of extravagant spending on antiques and other luxury items. In addition to her unbridled spending habits, she was a pretentious and demanding woman who was unrelenting in her criticisms of Henry, especially of his appearance.

In their classical marriage, each partner provided what the other one lacked. Henry had money and power, while Cynthia supplied beauty and refined taste. In spite of their efforts to keep their relationship alive by seeing several marriage therapists, in the end they disagreed on too many issues to make their bartered union work.

Unfortunately, it is only in the Land of Oz, where the scarecrow, the cowardly lion, and the tin man encounter the wizard, that there is any chance of getting the need for completion satisfied. There we might at least get medals for the brains, courage, and heart we so desire. In our real world, disappointment and frustration are likely to be the sole outcomes.

Another related motive that fuels romantic love is the need for validation. We fall in love with people who possess money, power, beauty, intelligence, and/or status because they make us look good. They make us look better than we are. Even though we realize that we will not be transformed by our partner's qualities, they are self-esteem boosts. "How could he get that gorgeous-looking gal?" and "How could she win that rich, brilliant, successful man?" are unspoken questions that circulate in the minds of our peers. While the specifics to the answers vary, the conclusions are the same: he must be more of a man than meets the eye and she must be smarter than she looks. We assume that the recipient of such good fortune has latent talents that are not apparent to the most discerning eye.

FAMILIAL ROLES

Other unconscious motives that come into play in romantic love are determined by familial roles. What role did we play in our families of origin? Were we the Hero, the Brilliant one, the Loser, the Lost Child (usually the middle child), the Boy/Girl Scout, the Mediator, the Caretaker (usually the oldest child), or the Baby of the Family? Whatever the role, it locked us into rigid ways of perceiving, thinking and behaving that limited our potential. This fact is especially true in dysfunctional families, where the children get drafted into meeting needs and handling functions that their parents were unable to fulfill.

In alcoholic families, for example, the alcoholic father or mother is far from an ideal parent. Even in the most benign alcoholic families—when the alcoholic parent is a quiet, non-abusive drunk—the alcohol addiction consumes time and energy that rightfully belong to the children and spouse. With one parent so thoroughly out of commission, the remaining spouse is left overwhelmed and depleted. As a result, their children's needs for security, safety, nurturance, encouragement, and affection are seldom met to any substantial degree.

Left to their own devices, the children in dysfunctional families frequently take on one of the missing functions in the family, such as caretaking or mediating, and as adults, they gravitate to similar roles. For example, a caretaking older daughter in an alcoholic family may fall in love with an insecure, heavy drinking man who needs lots of tending. While hoping for better outcomes this time around, adult children from alcoholic families are often so caught up in the earlier scenarios that they cannot extricate themselves from those powerful dynamics. They revert to the role they played early on in their families or identify with either parent's unhealthy coping strategy.

Similarly, children of divorced parents rely heavily on fantasy to make up for the missing ingredients in their families. If one parent literally or symbolically vanished from the family after a divorce, the absent parent is the one most likely to be embellished with the hopes and dreams of the children. As adults, then, the children seek out idealized versions of the absent caretaker for their romantic partners. When reality intervenes sometime later and they find out that their partners are as problematic, if not more so, than the parent who betrayed them, they become disillusioned.

SOUL MATES AND OTHER IDEALS

Idealization occurs regularly with children who grew up in divorced or unhappy families. Because the father is usually the absent parent, daughters in these families often idealize their fathers and try to find a replacement in a soul mate—someone to whom they can feel profoundly connected. While soul mates come in all sizes and shapes—they can be friends, lovers or relatives—they are most often romantic partners. They are people with whom there is an easy communication with deep empathic understanding, as if the relationship were made in heaven.

These soul mates are mirrors of our best selves in terms of beliefs, deep values, and feelings, and idealization makes them even more desirable. When a romantic union is based on this sort of shared connection, it is likely to last forever, a rare phenomenon indeed in our current culture. According to one estimate, these super relationships or super marriages are estimated to occur about 10 percent of the time[15].

One such super marriage showed up in a series of interviews of marital happiness. Rebecca, age forty-eight, and Jeff, age fifty-three, both from Jewish backgrounds, had been married for more than twenty-five years at the time of the interview. Almost carbon copies of one another, they had similar interests in art, literature, music, theater, politics, and ethnic restaurants. Admired by all their friends for their perfect marriage, they respected and admired one another and communicated easily about anything and everything, including their relationship. When conflicts arose, they said that they were able "to go beneath the surface," never screaming or yelling at one another. "Snarling," meaning being crabby and sarcastic, was as far as they would go.

What was clear from examining the interview data was that Rebecca married a father figure, a role Jeff was accustomed to playing in his own family, and Jeff married the witty, lively person life denied him when his father died unexpectantly. Jeff deeply admired Rebecca's quick wit and vitality; he called her a wisecrack artist. In fact, he was initially attracted

---

15   Harvey L. Ruben, *Super Marriage: Overcoming the Predictable Crises of Married Life,* New York: Bantam Books, 1986, p. 12.

to her when she was laughing and gesturing enthusiastically while talking to someone. Further underscoring the importance of this aspect of Rebecca's personality was her mother's comment that "Jeff's laughing at all her jokes was the glue that kept their marriage together."

As for Rebecca's attraction to Jeff, she missed a father figure in her life from the time of her parents' divorce when she was three years old, a loss she keenly felt. At the time of her parents' divorce, her father moved to a distant city and she seldom saw him thereafter. While both Rebecca and Jeff lost a parent before adulthood, Jeff's loss was much later chronologically. His father died when Jeff was in high school. As a result, he was better prepared to be a parental replacement than Rebecca would have been.

At the time of his father's death, Jeff, who was a serious, responsible guy without his father's sense of humor, became a father figure for his bereaved mother and sister. We therefore have two similar souls in background, values, and interests coming together with underlying, compatible needs and good communication skills to make for an ideal romantic relationship. Rebecca got a father figure, and Jeff got the lively, funny partner he wanted.

PSYCHOLOGICAL INCOMPATIBILITY

Unfortunately, the likelihood of two people having Jeff and Rebecca's psychological compatibility is small. Ordinarily after the initial glow of romantic passion has faded, couples begin to experience less sexual and overall satisfaction with the relationship, unless some other bonding factor is in place. With individuals younger than twenty-five, for example, both partners may be looking for great love and understanding, but along with that desire they are hoping for a magical genie to take care of their day-to-day needs. In their quest for enduring love, they are often oblivious to the mundane aspects of living together, such as earning income, paying bills, cooking meals, cleaning the house, and taking out the garbage—life functions that parents routinely take care of. These reality demands often prove to be the undoing of their relationship.

In marriages of younger people, arguments about household chores regularly elicit misunderstanding, hurt feelings, name-calling, disillusionment, and disengagement that can lead to a romantic relationship's ending. Incidentally, marriages between partners younger than twenty-five are most likely to end in divorce in the United States.

Psychological incompatibility is also evident in situations where there is a generational age disparity of twenty years or more, as when a middle-aged man marries a much younger woman. He may be trying to recapture his youth, only to find that she is a demanding, self-centered adolescent who is seldom emotionally available. She, on the other hand, may have been hoping to be adored endlessly just like her father had adored her, only to discover a grumpy, aging man who complains a lot about her unavailability. For them both, their underlying hopes and dreams get dashed by reality. In other situations, both partners may have been hoping for a parental replacement, a more consistent and loving mother or father than they had, only to find childish and irresponsible features they had not counted on in their partner.

Reality can be a cruel teacher that exposes the fault lines in our own personalities and in those of our partners.

PSYCHOLOGICAL VULNERABILITY: A PREDISPOSING FACTOR

Emotional Intensity is another key factor affecting romantic love. When we are in the throes of strong emotions, we are psychologically vulnerable and more likely to fall in love. A classical study conducted in the 1970s[16] demonstrated how fear magnifies interpersonal attraction. In this study, subjects walking across a shaky, unstable bridge found the individuals on the other side more attractive than when walking across a safe, very steady bridge.

Psychological vulnerability is likely to occur after severe losses, including parental death, divorce, rejection by an important lover, or significant failures such as school or job dismissals. As a result of such a loss, we may be anxious, lonely, depressed, and depleted of self-esteem. In need of loving concern, we will be especially appreciative of the attention showered upon us by the next available suitor who appears on our doorstep.

In such a context the stage is set for rebound love to develop, and it frequently does. Because psychologically vulnerable people are hungry for love, they are less likely to be discerning about the personal characteristics of an attentive suitor. Looking for love indiscriminately, the vulnerable person is grateful for the attention and is eager to reciprocate. The desperate desire to be "in love" can be the catalyst for the beginning of a romantic relationship, but whether it lasts will be a function of their shared values and other sustaining factors.

Loneliness, anxiety, and depression, when they are not debilitating, also contribute to romantic love's intensity. For

---

16 Donald G. Dutton & Arthur P. Aron, "Some Evidence for Heightened Sexual Attraction Under Conditions of High Anxiety," *Journal of Personality and Social Psychology,* 30 (1974), pp.510-517.

example, when we are worried about the biological clock running out, we are more likely to get involved with someone we would have rejected at an earlier point in life. Our intense desire to have children colors our perception and appreciation of any interested party. The boring suitor is more likely to be viewed as loving and intelligent rather than uninteresting. When viewed through this new lens, his reserve and lack of spontaneity become less important. Psychological vulnerability does not necessarily distort reality, but it changes the configuration so that certain qualities stand out while others recede in importance. Our vulnerability colors our perceptions and makes them compatible with our needs of the moment.

FIRST LOVES

In adolescence—a time of first loves—we are all extremely vulnerable. Not only are sexual feelings super-charged at this time, but we also don't know what to do with them. Our changing bodies with new sensitive erogenous zones are confusing, and as a result we are awkward in our movements and interactions. One woman recalled how unsure of herself she was at age sixteen about conversing with a young man that she reverted to reading street and store signs throughout their first date. "Oh, there's Morgan Street" and "Here's Macy's" were the only topics of conversation that came to mind, and he did not do any better. Easily humiliated and unsure about how to navigate in adolescence, we stumble about our worlds until we meet the person who most captures our imagination, and then, when the surge of overwhelming romantic attraction hits us, and especially if it is reciprocated, we walk around on cloud nine.

Novelty, unpredictability, idealization, and merger fantasies—the desire to be one with our beloved—provide fertile ground for the development of passion. Whether it is a first crush—adoring someone from afar—or a full-blown romantic interaction, first loves are imbued with much emotional intensity. Just like firsts of all kinds—first day at school, first friend, first sexual experience, first day at college—first loves are special and stand out in memory and importance. Novelty is one of the ingredients that cements experience in memory.

While there are many stories about how well first loves work out, even after long separations and several marriages, the disappointing stories far outnumber the ones with happy endings. Unfortunately, the disappointing ones do not make the tabloids. One woman in therapy recounted the story of how her first love reappeared on her doorstep after a fifty-year absence. His wife of many years had died several years earlier, at which point he began searching for his lost love on the Internet . When he walked into his old flame's office for a luncheon meeting they had arranged by email, she was shocked at his changed appearance. His gorgeous curly hair was gone (he was totally bald), and he walked with a marked limp.

Besides the dramatic changes in appearance, he had become a gambler in his spare time, an avocation she detested, and during lunch he talked nonstop about himself, a personality trait she had once adored but now found disquieting. Throughout the lunch meeting and thereafter, she kept wondering what she had seen in him fifty years earlier. The intense passion of her adolescence and early adulthood had thoroughly vanished over time, leaving not even a trace of its energy on her present-day psyche. She had changed dramatically over the fifty years, while he had basically stayed the same.

When they first met, she was eighteen and he was twenty-five. He was the nephew of the owner of the car agency where she worked after high school graduation. He was an older, good-looking, sophisticated "man about town," and she was an attractive, intelligent, and naïve adolescent who had never ventured far from home. Their love affair lasted four years or so until he ended it, ostensibly because of religious differences. While she was initially devastated by the breakup, she got married several years later and was happily married, had four children, and was a successful writer. They never saw each other again except for that one luncheon reunion fifty years after their relationship ended.

LOVE AT FIRST SIGHT

As for love at first sight—that turbulent surge of sexual/emotional energy aroused by the stranger across the crowded room—the successful liaisons make interesting Valentine's Day stories, while the many unhappy ones disappear into the wastebasket for failed relationships. Frequently the subject of poems, music, literature, and movies, love at first sight is often described as sudden, intense, and cataclysmic.

Toni Morrison,[17] a winner of the Nobel Prize for Literature, wrote in her novel *Love* about the upheaval of infatuation, which is what she calls it: "The magic ax that chops away the world in one blow, leaving only the couple standing there trembling? Whatever they call it, it leaps over anything, takes the biggest chair, the largest slice, rules the ground wherever it walks, from a mansion to a swamp, and its selfishness is its beauty. Before I was reduced to singsong, I saw all kinds of mating. Most are two-night stands trying to last a season. Some, the riptide ones, claim exclusive right to the real name, even though everybody drowns in its wake."

Where does all this emotion come from? Clearly, it does

---

17   Toni Morrison, *Love*, New York: Vintage Books, 2003, 63 (paperback).

not come from intimate knowledge of the person in question, because we know very little at the time of first meeting.
All we really know is that the object of our dreams exudes a
familiar or longed-for quality. We might say that it was her
beautiful smile or his confident, masculine appearance or her
seductive manner that knocked us off our feet, but in fact, the
surge of feeling triggered by one or two traits in our partner
arises from the wellspring of unconscious yearnings, unresolved conflicts, significant values, and interests coupled with
the biological, procreative imperative. Out of this mixture of
hopes and desires, we create a fantasy that colors our perceptions and thoughts about this new love possibility. The fantasy
lasts as long as reality does not burst the bubble by providing
contradictory information too difficult to ignore.

THE CEMENT OF LONG-
TERM RELATIONSHIPS

What keeps the fires burning in those romantic unions
that last forever? A common passion—whether in the arts,
science, family, or religion—is one of the factors that keep
a relationship alive and prevents it from growing stale. The
common passion, or interest, enhances the relationship, providing both pleasure and satisfaction. If both members of the
pair love science, for example, their discussions and activities
related to science are intellectually stimulating for them both
and mutually gratifying. Not only do they find pleasure in
spending time with one another but also the activities themselves provide enjoyment.

If a common interest is going to function as a sustaining
factor in the relationship, however, it needs to be central in
importance to both partners. Going to the movies together

might be fun, but it typically does not qualify as a bonding ingredient for most couples unless they are both film critics or really adore movies. Similarly, if both partners are of the same religion, which is generally a *plus* in terms of compatibility, religion will be a sustaining factor only if both partners share a deep commitment to it. Being of the same religion is not enough on its own to keep two unhappy romantic partners together for the long haul.

SIMILARITY AND BEST FRIENDS

Similarity is a major sustaining factor in romantic relationships. Being of the same cultural/family background, ethnicity, and religion provide a common basis for understanding the world and less opportunity for conflict to emerge. The literature on happy couples is clear: satisfied partners are more alike than different on many dimensions.[18] They are more similar than dissimilar in attitudes, personality, and physical attractiveness. They also tend to agree more with each other and have similar interests. While the popular maxim that opposites attract has some validity insofar as initial attraction is concerned, similarity is clearly the more stabilizing factor over time.

Carol, fifty-five, and Mark, sixty, had similar family values, friends, and backgrounds, but were quite different in terms of personality and interests. Mark was the outgoing, rugged salesman who enjoyed boating, fishing, hunting, and politics, while Carol was the introverted churchgoer who devoted her life to charity projects and other religious activities, such as singing in the choir and Sunday school teaching. Religion

---

18 Geraldine K. Piorkowski, *Too Close for Comfort: Exploring the Risks of Intimacy*, Cambridge, MA: Perseus Publishing (paperback), 1994, p. 267.

was not a bonding factor for their marriage, but neither was it a source of conflict, because although he seldom went to church, she was not bothered by his non-attendance.

Besides the couple's disparate interests, they were also different in temperament. Carol was an even-tempered, easy-going person who retreated into silence when hurt, while Mark was the loud, expressive one who would bellow in outrage. Regardless of their differences, however, they considered each other "best friends" and were able to talk through their conflicts. Their only restriction on honesty was their cardinal rule never to say anything they would later regret. "Never, never have we called each other a name," he said. He believed as his mother did, "Sugarcoat your words, because you'll never know when you'll have to eat them."

Initially Mark was attracted to Carol's "knock-out looks" and Carol was attracted to Mark's fun-loving personality. He also admired her religious commitments, even though he himself was not so inclined. At the time they met, Carol was recovering from the death of her father, to whom she was quite close, and Mark provided much-needed comic relief. In addition, he had a wide circle of friends who were a source of comfort and social interaction for Carol. At the beginning, therefore, they met each other's underlying psychological needs and values.

Even though Mark and Carol had different personalities and interests, what kept them together over the next thirty-three years, they said, was similarity. They grew up in the same neighborhood and continued to live in that same area with their children. They both valued *family*, and much of their social life centered around family life and high school friendships. They did have some interests in common, such as sailing, dancing, dinner outings, and joint activities with their children (scouting and sports), that provided much pleasure to them both, and they did talk a lot to one another. Their happy marriage would have gone on forever, but Mark died suddenly of a heart attack in his mid-sixties, leaving a distraught Carol to find her own way in a social world filled with family and close friends. After Mark's death, she was able to continue her charitable and social activities on familiar ground, thereby receiving considerable emotional support in the process.

DIFFERENT VERSIONS OF ROMANTIC LOVE

In earlier centuries, romantic love was fueled by power and status considerations, especially among the nobility. Such mergers, including arranged marriages, were based on overall benefit to the family, the tribe, and/or the nation. Monarchs intent on expanding their empires chose romantic partners with their acquisitive desires in mind. In the modern age, power and status appear to have less overt influence, but they still operate, both consciously and unconsciously, to affect partner choice. Modern love seekers continue to fall in love to improve their social and/or financial status, and gold-diggers run rampant in all modern cultures.

In modern Eastern and African countries where arranged marriages ruled the world of romance for centuries, the semi-arranged marriage has replaced the old tradition, especially within more educated circles. Now matchmakers in the more modern, non-Western countries screen potential partners based on suitability, much like some dating sites in the West. *Suitability* refers to similar background, educational level, social status, values, and religion, all of which contribute to marital stability. In those countries, once a matchmaker has found a suitable prospect, it is up to the couple itself to decide if there is enough sexual and emotional attraction to make the relationship work. The final choice of marital partner is usually given to the potential bride and groom.

Based upon divorce statistics, marriages in modern Eastern and African countries fare better than those in the West; however, the unacceptability of divorce in these countries relative to its universal acceptance in the West and their more unreliable means of recording marriage and divorce transactions make it difficult to determine how well their marriages are really doing.

IN SUMMARY

In the initial phase, romantic love is not reliable, trustworthy, or dependable because the primary ingredients that fuel romantic love—novelty, fantasy, and emotional arousal—are transitory, easily stirred up, quick to diminish, and unconsciously-motivated. In addition, our imaginations so embellish the person we love with positive qualities that we are in danger of being blindsided by his/her unpredictability, short fuse, immaturity, or irrationality. "Smoke gets in your eyes," as the old love song goes, and it clouds our judgment until reality sets in. When the mask of fantasy falls off, we are left with an ordinary person, not an ideal.

Besides those considerations, we really are not sure what we are looking for in a partner, especially the first time around. We may tell ourselves that we're looking for a person with substantial values, a person of integrity, but underneath it all, it may be his good looks that turn us on and make us feel more attractive and lovable than usual.

In old India the prevailing philosophy regarding romantic

love was "First you marry; then you fall in love." While their implied advice about marrying blindly seems foolish, Indian sages were trying to warn us that we are on safer ground when we know someone well.

What then will sustain a romantic union that may have been built on shaky ground? Clearly, the bonding factors for romantic relationships are among the following: affection (really liking the person), companionship (enjoying being together), emotional responsiveness (sensitivity to one another's feelings), friendship, religious commitment, shared interests, trust, and unifying values, and the more of these qualities, the better for the relationship.

Communication skills, including the ability to resolve conflict, an equitable distribution of labor, and mutual sexual satisfaction are also vital in keeping a relationship healthy, no matter how badly it started. Being similar rather than different, especially around attitudes and values, gives the relationship a big boost in the right direction. While being blinded initially is par for the course, it is important to discover as soon as we can whether a romance has enough staying power to last forever, if that is what we want.

CHAPTER 4

Vulnerable People Are More Likable Than Super-Confident Ones

SOMEONE ONCE ASKED me whether as a psychologist I had ever disliked any of my patients. I answered honestly that I had not. Because most of the patients I had seen over the years come into psychotherapy voluntarily, they tend to be unmasked and free of defenses. They come into therapy because their worlds are falling apart and they are in crisis. In psychotherapy most patients are not pretentious or arrogant but painfully honest about what is wrong with their lives, and as a result they tug at our heartstrings. They are vulnerable people.

WHAT IS HEALTHY VULNERABILITY?

Vulnerability is an openness about feelings, successes, failures, strengths, and inadequacies as well as hopes and dreams. It is honesty without defensiveness. A person comfortable being vulnerable can talk as easily about the disappointment of not getting a desired promotion as about the pleasure of finally getting that long-desired, dream house. Being vulnerable is being authentic or genuine.

Healthy vulnerability excludes the mentally ill, whose vulnerability is tragically apparent, and chronic complainers, who wear their ailments like a badge of honor. Chronic complainers are manipulators who use their negativity as a defense; they want to keep people away. Because of this strategy, they seldom engage with others about what they enjoy in life.

VULNERABILITY IS A MIXED BAG

Vulnerability itself, even the healthy variety, is risky. Sometimes when we are vulnerable—when we are exposed with our weaknesses laid bare—we get hurt. As a result, vulnerability is a stance that we generally reserve for our most trustworthy friends. For the rest of the world, we use our persona, or public personality, to navigate our social and professional worlds.

While vulnerability is dangerous, it is also endearing. We are most touched by and open to the most defenseless among us. For example, babies are universally loved, and young children who lack the guile and sophistication of adults can easily charm us with their naturalness and exuberance. Their vulnerability is both engaging and powerful. Similarly, adults who retain a childlike innocence and playfulness are appealing and likable.

We tend to like people who are spontaneous—the ones with whom we can easily laugh. The comedians who poke fun at themselves are likable, as are the so-called life-of-the-party types. Besides the fun-loving people, we also like people who wear their hearts on their sleeves and talk openly about their heartaches. Country singers strumming their guitars, lamenting their lost loves, are also likable. In all these situations, we can identify with their stories, both the funny, self-disparaging anecdotes and the sad, depressing tales.

While Western society imbues self-confidence with high status and desirability, and it is clearly valuable, vulnerability is easier to relate to and more likely to foster intimacy. Besides being more likable, vulnerable people are more trustworthy, nonthreatening, and noncompetitive. Because of their honesty, we know where they are coming from, where they stand. As a result, we can relax and lower our defenses.

In contrast, we admire and respect super-confident people, but we do not necessarily like them. While we may wish that some of their self-confidence would rub off on us, we are also wary of them. We typically keep them at an emotional distance where we can observe them and don't readily share our vulnerabilities with them. Our distrust is based not exclusively on envy, but rather on the suspicion that no one can be that self-confident all the time. Often our suspicions are correct, because many super-confident types hide significant vulnerabilities under an armor of bravado. Among the confident-appearing types who have difficulty being vulnerable are narcissists, blamers, conflict avoiders, oppositional types, passive-aggressive personalities, emotional hermits, immature types, and drama queens.[19]

---

19 Geraldine K. Piorkowski, *Adult Children of Divorce: Confused Love Seekers,* Westport, CT: Praeger, 2008.

NARCISSISTS

With super-confident-appearing people, especially the arrogant or pretentious ones, we feel uncomfortable and intimidated. Even a haughty salesclerk with a dismissive manner can threaten our self-confidence. After a brief interchange we often wind up feeling annoyed and unimportant. The self-imposed sense of superiority of such a narcissist communicates both elevated status and disdain for those of us with lesser credentials.

The attempts of the narcissist to impress us with a lengthy list of famous acquaintances or a travelogue of world-renowned journeys generally fail to impress us. We stop listening to their name and place dropping because our lesser accomplishments pale in comparison, and we feel inadequate. We have trouble understanding or identifying with others whose background, talents, or knowledge are beyond our experience, particularly the boastful ones. We may have to socialize with them as part of our work responsibilities, but we don't typically include them in our intimate circles.

Narcissists are difficult people to have as friends or intimate partners. Because they are primarily concerned with their own thoughts and feelings, they are poor listeners. They are not interested in what other people are saying, and as a result they dominate conversational domains. When the other person in the conversation shifts gears and introduces a new topic, narcissists may listen politely for a few minutes, but their lack of interest is apparent when after a few seconds of feigned attention, they revert to their favorite activity, talking about themselves.

Narcissists have inordinate difficulty with vulnerability. Acknowledging shortcomings or failures is a shameful admission of inadequacy for them, and they respond angrily when a personality or intellectual flaw is exposed. For example, one elderly narcissistic woman when asked by a relative about her daughter's birth date furiously replied, "How am I supposed to remember such trivial things?" Obviously her memory failure was a narcissistic injury to her in that it revealed a chink in her armor of superiority. She could not acknowledge a memory lapse common to senior citizens, because the admission was a sign of imperfection. Most of her life she had been successful in keeping her flaws hidden under a narcissistic veneer and resented any attention that suggested that she was less than ideal. Underneath her protective armor, she, like most narcissists, had very low self-esteem.

BLAMERS AND CONFLICT AVOIDERS

Like narcissists, both blamers and conflict avoiders avoid vulnerability by denying responsibility for errors or failures. While all three groups are quick to blame others for misdeeds, blamers and conflict avoiders are much less self-absorbed than narcissists. They can both be sensitive and thoughtful when there is smooth sailing, but their shortcomings are dramatically evident when conflict arises on the interpersonal scene.

In conflictual arenas—when there is disagreement or mistakes in judgment—blamers are quick to point out their partners' faults. They seldom say "I'm sorry" or ask for forgiveness, and as a result, they come across as invincible and invulnerable, qualities that do not lend themselves to closeness. They tend to be angry, judgmental individuals quick to assign responsibility for negative outcomes to someone else. Even in extreme situations, such as a violent assault on a wife or partner, domestic abusers will blame their partner for making them angry and instigating the violence. "If she hadn't raised her voice or questioned my authority," he rationalizes, "I wouldn't have hit her." Most perpetrators of domestic violence are clearly blamers.

The conflict avoider, on the other hand, is a more passive, benign person who has low tolerance for disagreements. Having grown up in angry households where nothing got resolved, they go to inordinate lengths to avoid confrontations. Interpersonal tranquility is where they prefer to bask, a place where nothing threatens their self-esteem.

Whenever a discussion is on the verge of overt conflict, avoiders change the subject to a more neutral one. Sometimes their attempts to shift gears are transparent, as when they look out the window and point out objects of interest on the distant horizon, while at other times, their distracting antics are more subtle. When subtle, the change of topic may be tangentially related to the conflictual area, but without the emotional power of the original. For example, changing a discussion of current politics to the political life of the eighteenth century is a diversion that might be used to put the interactions on safer ground.

OPPOSITIONAL TYPES AND THE PASSIVE-AGGRESSIVE PERSONALITY

Oppositional types have an inordinate need to be in control and manage to do so by contradicting others, correcting them, or by using humor, especially puns, to avoid being vulnerable. Because they view others as challengers or competitors, they are wary of others and on the lookout for opportunities to disarm them verbally. Often they interrupt the other person's story with an opposing point or they nitpick with un-essential details, such as, "No, it happened on a Tuesday, not a Thursday," as if the integrity of the anecdote depended on absolute precision of detail. Skilled at one-upmanship, they want to be on top, where they are clearly less vulnerable. Pulling the rug out from under their opponents is a favorite strategy.

Oppositional types' use of humor, while engaging, is de-signed to change topics from serious, potentially threatening areas to lighter, less dangerous ones. Like the court jesters of old, oppositional types are adept at shifting the focus of discussion from war and strife to more amusing concerns. By turning a serious moment into laughter, they seize control of the situation, and in the process earn the applause of their audience. We are all bemused by humor and find it not only entertaining but relaxing to boot. Their oppositional strategy is successful at avoiding warfare while earning kudos at the same time.

The passive-aggressive personality is another personality type with inordinate difficulty being vulnerable. Rather than telling someone directly about their disappointments and risk being attacked in return, they instead rely on subtle, dif-fuse means of confronting perceived enemies. Obfuscation, the strategy of blinding or confusing his opponents, is their primary weapon. They forget their promises, lie, sulk, and/or procrastinate their commitments to avoid pleasing the de-manding and/or ungrateful boss or partner.

Intimate partners who are passive-aggressive often have chronic difficulty meeting their responsibilities. Because they typically fail to perform assigned household chores, from tak-ing out the garbage to paying bills on time, they create chaos in the daily operation of the household. Pleading ignorance or forgetfulness, they come across as misunderstood victims of undue stress who also may drink too much. In this scenario, the overworked partner can become frantic and then exhausted, trying to meet all the needs and demands of the family before deciding to exit. Or else the overworked partner may stick around—a bitter and unhappy person, depleted of energy and resources, who cannot envision or commit to an alternative way of living.

EMOTIONAL HERMITS

Emotional hermits may look like strong, silent, confident types, but appearances are deceiving. In the interpersonal world, they are lonely people who prefer to avoid relationships altogether because relationships are far too emotionally dangerous for them. More adept in the world of ideas and concepts than of feelings, emotional hermits are often intelligent, talented scholars, bankers, engineers, doctors, lawyers, or other professionals. While preferring solitude, emotional hermits are occasionally swept off their feet by intense feelings of sexual attraction and become anxious about losing control. When this happens, they feel very vulnerable and unsure of themselves.

Their occasional forays into emotional entanglement end poorly most of the time. Because emotional hermits lack interpersonal skills in close relationships, they get confused when the other person makes demands or temporarily withdraws from the relationship. These shifts in relatedness are baffling to them, and they often retreat from a potentially meaningful relationship even before it gets serious. Because of their own insecurities, emotional relationships are alien to them. Either they grew up in an emotionally repressed household where feelings were seldom talked about or in a volatile family, where emotions led to explosive and unpredictable behavior. In either case, emotionally close relationships are not safe for emotional hermits.

IMMATURE TYPES

Other personalities that have difficulty being vulnerable but may appear confident are immature types. They come in all shapes and sizes, from Peter Pan and Cinderella who never grew up to Don Juan and Jezebel, intent on conquest. For whatever the developmental reason, the emotional maturity of immature personalities has not kept up with their chronological ages and they are stuck repeating earlier developmental scripts.

Both Peter Pan and Cinderella want to spend all their time in Neverland, where the responsibilities of adulthood are banished forever. Peter Pan enjoys playing athletic or video games in adulthood, while Cinderella, a more passive creature, sits around waiting for Prince Charming to show up. Primarily interested in pleasure and same-sex activities, such as sporting events, Peter Pans spend hours playing cards, hanging around the bars, playing golf, and/or drinking with the boys.

Cinderellas, on the other hand, are highly invested in the fantasy of romantic love, believing that their lives will be transformed once the man of their dreams arrives on the scene. Because they feel highly inadequate as a grown-up, both Peter Pan and Cinderella hide their vulnerability under child-like exteriors. While both Cinderella and Peter Pan are similar, her lack of ambition and dependency are more socially acceptable than his irresponsible behaviors.

Don Juans and Jezebels are more exploitative personalities

and less trustworthy than the Peter Pans and Cinderellas of the world. In their arsenal of defensive strategies, they use sex as their main weapon, with seduction being the goal. Since they derive excitement and validation from the conquest and not the relationship, they lose interest quickly and are ready to move on once the seduction is complete.

Because emotional closeness resulted in betrayal or abandonment in the past, ongoing intimacy is unreliable and conflict-ridden for Don Juan and Jezebel, so they sample intimacy for brief periods of time before becoming restless and ending the relationship. The casualties of such maneuvers are their unsuspecting partners, many of whom were looking for a long-term relationship and instead wind up devastated at its abrupt ending.

DRAMA QUEENS

Drama queens may be female or male, and they represent another exploitative group, but rather than using sex to manipulate others, they use feelings (with a capital F) to get what they want. Their emotional life with its ups and downs is always on center stage. When they are upset, everybody around is duly informed. When they are happy, their exuberance is heard all over their world. Somewhat hysterical and adept at hyperbole, they dress dramatically to command attention. Because they are lively and interesting, they have no difficulty attracting friends and romantic partners.

The problem with drama queens, however, is that their partners wind up feeling used. Because drama queens are adept at manipulating others, their partners' voices get drowned out by all the drama. In the middle of the psychological chaos generated by drama queens, their rational partners have little chance of getting their needs met. In contrast to the drama queen, the partner easily blends into the woodwork.

Akin to narcissists, drama queens are also highly self-serving. The difference between them lies in the amount of shared vulnerability. Typically, drama queens expose more vulnerability than the more emotionally controlled narcissist, and as a result, tend to be more likable.

THE RISKS OF VULNERABILITY

If vulnerability is so appealing, why do we share so little of ourselves with others? Essentially because of the risks to our self-esteem. We do not want to be hurt, rejected, laughed at, disappointed, betrayed, criticized, shamed, or made to feel guilty. We do not want to feel helpless or overwhelmed by the negative reactions of others in response to our life stories. In short, no matter how rewarding honesty and genuineness can be, vulnerability may appear too dangerous.

We may fear that we will be humiliated after we have disclosed an especially shameful experience. After such sharing, we may worry that we will be viewed as naïve, immature, stupid, or even worse, that we will be perceived as neurotic or perverted and that others will avoid our company. We fear the negative opinions of other people—their thinking less of us—and their disrespect.

We also fear negative repercussions down the road from being honest. Revealing our worst failing to another person could result in that failure getting thrown back in our face months or even years later: "Yes, you really are crazy or stupid or self-centered." If the feared outcome occurs, we will feel hurt, exposed, and betrayed by our friend's or partner's callous insensitivity and reluctant thereafter to trust that person again.

In our night dreams, our fears of humiliation show up in images of being exposed in some way—discovered naked or sitting on the toilet. One man feared closeness because, as he said, "They will find out that underneath all that tinsel is more tinsel." In other words, he feared that he was a phony throughout; that he was all glitter with no substance.

Fears of being betrayed are quite common. When we trust someone and then find out that we were fed a bunch of lies, we feel like a fool. We feel naïve and stupid to have believed someone whose credibility is a sham. In intimate relationships, the betrayal usually centers on sexual fidelity. Finding out that we were cheated on is a blow, not only to our self-confidence, but also to our sexual identity. We may worry that we are not sexually attractive enough to hold onto a partner and never will be.

Another risk of being vulnerable is that of losing control and feeling helpless. Letting a significant friend or partner know how lonely or upset we are may result in their becoming too intrusive. For example, telling someone that we are feeling depressed may lead to too many phone calls inquiring about our well-being and too many unwanted drop-ins. Our sense of autonomy, our need to be our own person, may feel violated. As a result, we may feel intruded upon or smothered by the excessive attention. Feeling helpless, not knowing what to say or do, is uncomfortable, which is why it is so much easier to help someone than be helped.

Disappointment is another common risk of being vulnerable. While we had hoped to be understood when we shared a personally intimate experience, the other person's reaction may add to our upset. The person may be indifferent, angered, or critical as a result of what we related. The indignant question, "How could you have ____?" adds insult to injury, and we wind up further determined not to share our vulnerabilities with anyone.

Perhaps the most painful fear of being vulnerable is the fear of rejection. We do not want others to know what we're ashamed of or feel guilty about, lest they turn their backs on us and walk away. In contrast to salespeople who are inured to day-to-day rejection, most of us feel deeply hurt when we are rejected by others, especially the people we value. Rejection takes a chunk out of our self-worth and leaves us questioning ourselves—our values, personality, decisions, and behavior.

THE REWARDS OF SHARING VULNERABILITY

Even though sharing vulnerabilities with others is risky, it is the quickest and most reliable pathway to close, meaningful relationships in adulthood. While it does require courage and good judgment, letting close friends and romantic partners know who we are, warts and all, is the best antidote to loneliness. Such sharing enriches our lives and leaves us feeling more at peace with ourselves. It is a means of integrating our inner and outer worlds and keeping psychological demons at bay. The demons of addiction, chronic anxiety, anger, compulsions, depression, and a whole host of stress-related diseases lose their potency when we are in warm, emotionally intimate relationships.

The sharing of our vulnerabilities reaps other social rewards as well. We are more likely to be liked by others, our acquaintances, coworkers, and neighbors, if we are spontaneous and authentic rather than boastful and pretentious. Others are more likely to identify with us, find us more relatable and less threatening than people who have defensive personalities. Interpersonal honesty facilitates emotional attachments in both friendship and romantic love.

Degrees of Closeness

Talking about the more superficial aspects of our lives—our attitudes, interests, and opinions about art, food, literature, movies, music, the neighborhood, politics, religion, restaurants, sports, television, and work—is the easiest way to begin and maintain emotionally close relationships. Most of us are reasonably comfortable in talking about such topics without feeling that we are revealing too much. As a result of such sharing, we establish personal relationships with some degree of closeness.

When we share the more personal aspects of ourselves—our successes and failures, our strengths and weaknesses, our most important values, our hopes and dreams, our feelings about our lives, and most intimately, the secrets in our lives, which ordinarily are reserved for therapists and confessors alike—we often get anxious about being hurt, betrayed, or criticized. When shared judiciously, though, when a degree of trust has been established, the benefits of greater emotional intimacy far outweigh the dangers.

Daily Sharing

While being able to talk with someone daily about each day's joys and tribulations, including the feelings that dominated the day, is rare in this technological age, such an exercise is worth pursuing in person, by phone, or by social media. Using e-mails, facebook, and texts does provide personal information but they sadly lack nonverbal cues (facial expression, tone of voice) and are therefore short on feelings.

Being able to respond to a friend or coworker who asks how we are with honest feelings like, "I've had a bad day. My computer was down, and I didn't accomplish a thing," or "I'm worried about my mother. She seems to be getting worse" is the quickest way to connect to another person, and if one's friend responds with empathy, the conversation is off to a meaningful start.

Besides the benefit of feeling less stressed after such sharing, there are other insights to be gained. We learn, for example, that others, even the most confident appearing among us, have bad days filled with worry and frustration. We learn that we are not alone in the world, that pain and suffering are part of the human condition, and that we suffer less when in the company of compassionate friends.

IN SUMMARY

Too often we spend a great deal of energy trying to appear super adequate or perfectly competent. This drive for perfection is not only time-consuming but also fraught with disappointment. We are, after all, fallible creatures. When a somewhat pompous clergyman was told by his spiritual advisor, "Fear not; you *are* inadequate," he felt surprisingly relieved. In that instant, he became profoundly aware that he could not handle every situation perfectly. All he could do was his best, and even that might not be good enough in all situations. Accompanying this realization was a profound sense of freedom, the freedom to stop worrying about perfection and genuinely be himself.

In this computer and cell phone age where loneliness abounds, the sharing of vulnerabilities—being authentic—does not come easy. Many personalities who are distrustful of others believe that false bravado and other masks of sanity are necessary to navigate the world. For them such protection is the safest option. Unfortunately, in the process of pursuing safety, they miss out on the genuine joys that friendship and romantic love can bring.

While the sharing of vulnerabilities is risky, it is the surest path to interpersonal closeness. Whether in friendship or romantic love, being open about feelings, failures, and accomplishments gives others permission to share at this same level of intimacy. And emotional intimacy with others is the best antidote to feelings of alienation and isolation.

CHAPTER 5

You Can't Make Anybody Do Anything

ONE OF THE high-profile cases I was involved with as a clinical psychologist dealt with a fifteen-year-old African American boy who shot and killed his brother. An important part of the determination of his sentence was the psychological evaluation, including the results of a battery of psychological tests I had to administer.

As soon as the young man entered the designated testing office, it was obvious from his nonverbal manner that he was in no mood to talk to me. He sat down on the floor, folded his arms across his chest, and stared at the floor with an angry expression on his face. Realizing how important my evaluation was to his sentencing, I tried every psychological strategy I knew to gain his cooperation, but after forty-five minutes I was having no luck at all, so I packed up my testing paraphernalia and said emphatically, "It is clear that I can't make you talk to me," and stood to leave.

When I was at the door, he shifted his posture, looked at me for the first time, and said, "What do you want to know?"

From that moment on, he was fully cooperative with the examination and testing procedures.

What changed his mind? Apparently it was his realization that he was in control of cooperating and that I could not make him do anything. My initial decision to end the session was not a ploy but was based on my frustration and helplessness. At the point I gave up, I was feeling like a failure at my assigned task, because I had exhausted my repertoire of psychological interventions and had nowhere to go. From his perspective he was probably feeling less pressure to perform at that time, so he gave up his stubborn resistance. He, like all of us, to one degree or another, was in control.

THE SENSE OF AUTONOMY

From the time we are about two years of age, our autonomy, or our ability to self-govern, becomes dramatically evident. Even though glimpses of autonomy are evident even earlier in the varying attentiveness and willfulness of younger babies, the toddler stage is the one where autonomy reigns supreme.

According to Erik Erikson, who wrote the classic text *Childhood and Society*,[20] the psychosocial stage of autonomy versus shame/doubt (ages eighteen months old to four years) is the developmental arena for children to test their growing self-determination. The age of "the terrible twos," when every request is met with a resounding "No," serves the important function of solidifying the sense of self.

We can walk, talk to some degree, and feed ourselves by this time, and we are becoming more adept at exercising our will during this stage. "No, I don't want to eat peas." "No, I

---

20   Erik H. Erikson, *Childhood and Society*, New York: Norton, 1950.

don't want to wear a coat." And especially, "No, I don't want to go to bed," is regularly heard. Only by opposing the will of our parents and other caretakers do we begin to strengthen our own resolve. When we go along with every environmental desire, we have a hard time differentiating ourselves from the people around us. Only by resistance can we feel our own strength.

Following a seminar on the developmental stages of children, a Hispanic man came up to the leader of the seminar tearfully expressing gratitude for the information. As the father of a healthy, vocal, and appropriately stubborn two-year-old son, he had begun to believe that his little son was intrinsically evil and destined for a life of crime. When he learned otherwise—that his son's behavior was a normal developmental phase and not a sign of recalcitrance or disrespect for adults—he was very relieved.

While this stage is particularly hard on parents, who may be concerned that their children will grow up to be tyrants, successful completion of this phase is important for the development of autonomy and self-esteem. When there is too much parental coercion or domination at this time, children are left feeling inadequate, ashamed of themselves, and filled with self-doubt because they have had too little opportunity to flex their own muscles.

COMMON WILLFULNESS IN CHILDREN

Children who are forced to behave in ways that are the opposite of their predilections develop their own brand of resistance. Some resistance tactics are relatively benign, like feeding despised vegetables to the dog under the table, brushing one's teeth carelessly, or putting away toys haphazardly.

Getting through disliked chores with as little effort as possible is a resistance strategy as old and widespread as childhood.

One four-year-old boy busily watching TV was often interrupted by his doting relatives eager to talk with him. Scolded repeatedly by his father for not looking away from the television set, facing his adoring relative, and making eye contact, he developed the habit of looking just past the relative, catching glimpses of the program, and continuing to daydream about the TV episode he wanted to watch. While his father could control his outward behavior to some extent, only the child had control of his attention and inner life.

In another situation, the educated, ambitious mother of a three-year-old boy came home from a seminar on early education eager to teach the alphabet to her firstborn child. While her very verbal child quickly devoured the alphabet-learning experience, he got stuck on the letter *H* and for months thereafter, appeared unable to learn that letter. The pressure on him to learn the alphabet was apparently so overwhelming that he resisted with one of the few tools he had at his disposal, namely, "forgetting." Whether his anxiety about getting the alphabet right prevented him from learning that particular letter or he was stubbornly exercising his autonomy is difficult to determine in a young child.

However, "forgetting" to do chores—whether it's homework, taking out the garbage or washing hands before dinner—is a common act of willfulness that is evident in all households, but most dramatically in angry, dominating ones. In families with controlling parents, children have little recourse for self-assertion except for devious resistance, and "forgetting" is one of those underhanded tactics that bewilders parents because its cause is not readily apparent.

Children who were physically abused have often described

in their journals their steely determination not to cry. Not willing to give their parent or caretaker the satisfaction of knowing that the abuse is having an effect, these children develop self-control strategies that give them the upper hand at one level. While their lack of response may further anger the abuser, these children derive satisfaction from their willful exercise of autonomy. Essentially they are communicating to the abuser, "You don't matter to me at all. Nothing you do can hurt me. You are impotent and insignificant."

With children, too much parental control leads to stubborn resentment, which defies the external pressure to conform and creates its own means of discharge. The resentful child may vocally rebel, kick the dog or the cat, or imagine a world where he controls the universe. Being a benign dictator in a fantasy universe as opposed to a demoniacal tyrant bent upon destruction is clearly the preferred adaptation to coercion.

DESTRUCTIVE AUTONOMY IN ADOLESCENCE

Besides the many destructive acts that adolescents are prone to, such as drug abuse, reckless driving, suicidal behavior, and vandalism, anorexia nervosa, a psychiatric disorder characterized by a refusal to maintain normal body weight and a distorted body perception, stands out dramatically as self-assertion gone awry. While all adolescents seem to go through adult versions of the terrible twos, the anorexic adolescent who refuses to eat sufficiently to maintain body weight and well-being is an extreme example. She is courting disaster on all fronts.

The anorexic adolescent, most often female, is intensely afraid of gaining weight and manifests a disturbed self-image, especially about the size and shape of her body. Even though she appears grossly underweight at the time of diagnosis, she believes that she is generally overweight or that specific body parts, mainly her abdomen, buttocks, and/or thighs, are too fat. In the face of many objective indicators loudly proclaiming that she is dangerously underweight, her obsession with weight gain will continue unabated unless there is successful therapeutic intervention.

What prompts a young teenager to refuse to eat normally even when her health is at stake? When death is just a doorstep away? When the scale, mirror, and the cessation of menses all state unequivocally that she is way too thin? Part of the answer is stubborn willfulness; that is, exercising her own will by going against the directives of the adults around her. She wants to be her own person, and the best way of doing that, she unwisely figures, is to resist their demands to eat.

While her self-destructive behavior may also be prompted by depression or another psychiatric disorder, she, like many other dysfunctional young women, most likely grew up in an over-controlling family where there were far too many dictates regarding eating, sleeping, bathing, and other bodily functions—a place where there were too few opportunities to be herself. As a result, being herself meant disregarding healthy behavior in favor of angry defiance—a combination of anger and willfulness that overrides self-preservation.

Cutters—adolescents who cut their wrists and/or other body parts—are another example of self-determination wrought at great expense to physical health. The self-destructive behavior of cutters seems to represent an attempt to experience one's self in a highly differentiated way. For example, one hospitalized adolescent after cutting herself said that she felt more alive afterward. Her wrist-cutting, which often followed conflictual encounters with her mother, served as a way of separating herself from a domineering mother with whom she was enmeshed. While such extreme behaviors are pathological, they attest to the strength of self-determination, even in the face of danger.

More commonly, drug abuse and other reckless acts, such as driving a car or motorcycle at high speed, represent an adolescent's pursuit of destructive autonomy. Unfortunately, these widespread behaviors can be just as lethal to young people as overt suicidal actions.

AUTONOMY AND CONTROL IN ROMANTIC RELATIONSHIPS

In romantic love, the desire to merge with a lover—wanting to be intertwined forever in body and soul—often accompanies romantic passion, especially in its beginning stages. But the merger fantasy has a short life and is ordinarily replaced by its opposite, the fear of suffocating, when too much closeness gets in the way of daily life.

The dance of intimacy[21]—getting close and then backing off—is the name of the intimacy dynamic in romantic love. We want eternal closeness at one level but then find it *too much* at another, so we vacillate, wanting more intimacy one moment, but then feeling uncomfortable and smothered, we seek distance moments later. The dance of intimacy is filled with ambivalence.

One woman in therapy, who was an identical twin, described her relationship with her husband as improved

---

21 Harriet G. Lerner, *The Dance of Intimacy: A Woman's Guide to Courageous Acts of Change in Key Relationships*, New York: Harper & Row 1989.

following an anxiety-ridden period of "too much closeness." She said, "Things are now more distant but healthier between the two of us; we are less entangled." With intense closeness she felt lost and unsure about her own identity. She could not tell whether her desires were her own or her husband's. Her sense of self got compromised in this all-consuming, emotional relationship that was too focused on his needs and not hers.

One of the main anxieties in romantic relationships is the fear of losing autonomy, of having no control. We fear that we will have to spend too much of our energy pleasing the other person—that we will have no say in the relationship and that our wishes will be ignored. We will have to go places we have no desire to visit, talk to people who are of no interest to us, and do things that are burdensome. We fear that there will be no time for ourselves and that our independence will be lost.

Because of this fear, we often become highly insistent on getting our own way. Whenever we feel that our partner has more power in the relationship, we will demand our fair share one way or another. In addition, we resent being told what to do. It undermines our autonomy as an adult, so we go out of our way to exercise our own will. If she wants the garbage taken out now, we will do it later. If he insists on sex right now, we'll plead a headache.

The more she nags and the more he insists, the less likely it is that either partner will get what is desired. Nagging especially leads to psychological deafness on the part of the recipient. In general, resistance in any form will rear its ugly head and fighting will begin.

When demands from our partner are intense, resentment increases and subterfuge occurs. Passive-aggressive tactics, such as procrastination, forgetting, lying, and hostile behavior, will take over, ensuring that nothing gets resolved. He does not like being told what to do, and she does not want to make love with someone who demands intimacy.

Too much yielding to partners in romantic relationships leads to resentment and too much winning leads to guilt or an inflated, unrealistic sense of superiority. Compromise based on a sense of fair play, that is, "I'll go to the ballgame with you, if you go to the art museum with me," is the only way of making a romantic relationship work over the long haul. Without such compromises, one partner 's needs may get lost in the shuffle and unhappiness will ensue for both partners. Bullies may appear to be the victors in romantic conflicts, but their submissive partners usually have their own powerful, if underhanded, ways of getting their voices heard.

IS PHYSICAL PUNISHMENT EFFECTIVE IN CONTROLLING CHILDREN?

Is physical punishment effective in controlling children without undesirable consequences? The answer is "No," with some exceptions. For example, spanking children, while temporarily effective in suppressing undesirable behavior, is likely to increase the children's aggressiveness when they are older. It also increases their deviousness, their tendency to engage in the punished behavior behind parents' backs. It is also ineffective in teaching a child responsibility and self-control.

Because of growing research on the harmful effects of spanking, the American Academy of Pediatrics[22] does not endorse spanking under any circumstances. The academy

---

22 American Academy of Pediatrics, "Effective Discipline to Raise Healthy Children: Policy Statement," *Pediatrics,* December 2018.

maintains that spanking may cause harm to a child by affecting normal brain development. Both corporal punishment and harsh verbal abuse, in which a child is shamed or made fearful, may elevate stress hormones and lead to changes in the brain's architecture. The academy also believes that corporal punishment is less effective with repeated use and makes discipline more difficult as the child gets older.

Why do parents spank or physically punish their children? Because it appears that punishment works, even though it does not. Children will avoid the punishing parent and inhibit the so-called bad behavior in their presence, but it does not mean that punishment weakens the behavior in question. In fact, physical pain is likely to create anger toward the punisher and thereby cloak the behavior in strong emotion that strengthens the behavior. Just as paying too much attention to a tic or stutter gives it additional energy, so too does spanking have the same strengthening effect on bad behavior.

The most common reason for spanking, however, is parents' understandable anger at their children's negative behavior. Uncontrolled and disobedient children elicit anger, but unfortunately parental anger also arouses anger in children. The best course of action in taxing situations, whenever parents can maintain their composure, is a clear, rational message that directly conveys the unacceptability of the behavior followed by appropriate deprivation of privileges or lack of reward.

WHAT ABOUT TORTURE?

In general, painful, aversive stimulation works in eliminating undesirable behavior when it is severe, applied immediately after the behavior, and occurs every time the behavior is elicited. As for torture, the results are mixed. Some military interrogators, for example, maintain that effective intelligence can be gained with torture, while others have testified that the gained information is often either inaccurate or just as accessible using more humane methods.[23] Methods classified as torture include harsh electrical shocks, amputation of body parts, shame-inducing strategies involving nudity and urination, and waterboarding. Sleep deprivation and being shackled nude in stress positions are other common, anxiety-arousing, and dehumanizing techniques.

While the efficacy of torture in producing worthwhile military information during wartime is unclear, what is dramatically evident is that torture has serious consequences for victims. Torture has profound physical and psychological effects that can last a lifetime. Besides the long-lasting effects on the victim, the victim's family and friends are also negatively impacted by torture. Family members and friends can suffer for years from the erratic behavior of the victim, which may include violent behavior directed toward them and middle-of-the-night awakenings with bone-chilling screams.

Among the common psychological symptoms that victims of torture suffer are increased anxiety, depression, nightmares, insomnia, memory lapses, social withdrawal, sexual dysfunction, and headaches. Often grouped together as post-traumatic stress disorder (PTSD), these symptoms loudly proclaim how painful and destructive traumatic experiences can be. Intense, stressful events, such as rape, torture, and wartime exposure, affect the neurological wiring of the brain and produce a host of physical disorders, along with psychological

---

23 R. Janoff-Bulman, "Erroneous Assumptions: Popular Belief in the Effectiveness of Torture Interrogation," *Peace and Conflict: Journal of Peace Psychology,* 13 (4), (2007), 429-435.

distress. The psychological effects especially can be profound, affecting judgment and rationality in victims forever.

FACTORS THAT INFLUENCE COMPLIANCE

From the time Stanley Milgram conducted his experiments on obedience to authority in the 1960s,[24] experimental evidence validated anecdotal evidence dating back centuries that people are capable of inflicting severe punishment on their fellow human beings on their own or when told to do so. In addition, a few years earlier, World War II witnessed the horrendous cruelty of the Nazis toward the Jews, gays, and gypsies, in effect validating man's inhumanity to man and the obedience of rank and file soldiers to higher authority.

In the Milgram experiment, participants were told to administer high levels of shock to "learners" for wrong answers on a memory test. While many of the volunteers had qualms about administering such high levels of shock, they continued to do so, even when the victims were ostensibly screaming from pain. Strong encouragement from a perceived legitimate authority overrode any qualms they had about continuing the shock, with 65 percent of the subjects administering the highest level of shock. It appeared that they went along with administering the punishment because they feared loss of status or respect, and they needed to be "good participants" or "good soldiers." In addition, like soldiers in combat, the people in the experiment felt that they were doing their duty and that the person in authority was the responsible one.

In a more recent replication of the Milgram experiments,[25]

---

24 Stanley Milgram, "Behavioral Study of Obedience," *Journal of Abnormal and Social Psychology*, 67 (4) (1963), 371-8.

25 Michael Shermer, "Shock and Awe," *Scientific American*, 307,5 (November 2012), 86.

however, it was found that most of the subjects did not exhibit blind obedience to authority but rather manifested deep moral conflict about hurting others. The investigator concluded, "Human moral nature includes a propensity to be empathetic, kind, and good to our fellow kin and group members, plus an inclination to be xenophobic, cruel, and evil to tribal others." Thus he was acknowledging both man's inhumanity to strangers and his benevolence to family and friends.

Besides obedience to authority figures, peer pressure is another factor that leads to immoral or cruel behavior that may be contrary to one's moral code. Fraternities and sororities are notorious for outlandish and harmful group behavior that a solitary member would be unlikely to commit. Forcing a pledge to consume large quantities of alcohol or food that can lead to serious impairment and even death is a tragic outcome that occurs all too frequently on the American college scene. In these instances, participants value their membership in the group more than they value their conscience or moral code.

In advertising designed to influence buying, several common techniques are used to make products more attractive. While advertisers cannot *make* anyone buy anything, they are skilled at lowering resistance to purchasing whatever they are selling. Initially they try to create a desire for the product and then they cite authority figures who legitimize the product, and as a follow up, they use one or more of the following advertising strategies: conformity (everyone is using it), commitment (a free trial or a great initial deal to get you hooked), and/or scarcity (not many are left). If our favorite TV or movie star is using it and our best friend swears by it, we feel the need to try it, at least.

IN SUMMARY

We all possess a steely sense of self that can resist any attempt at influence. From the age of two or thereabouts, our autonomy—our ability to self-govern—becomes apparent. We develop our identity and self-confidence as we explore our immediate world. Because our autonomy is such a precious gift, we innately resist all attempts to stifle it and feel resentful when the control is extreme. While others may be able to control our outward behavior, they cannot control the autonomous parts of ourselves, our minds and souls, with much success.

The temper tantrums and stubbornness of toddlers are a testament to the importance of autonomy. While temper tantrums typically vanish with time and maturity, stubbornness can remain forever as a personality or character trait. The more parental control exerted during childhood, the more likely it is that stubborn resentment will endure into adulthood and old age.

The adage "Choose your battles" is a wise directive that is especially relevant to this topic. While you cannot make anyone do anything without harmful repercussions or enduring resentment, there are obviously requirements for living that need to be enforced. It is wise to keep in mind, however, that appeals to our better nature and the loss of meaningful rewards are more effective in changing undesirable behavior than punishment, and positive reinforcement for good behavior works wonders. Whether we are dealing with a stubborn toddler, a belligerent teenager, or an intransigent romantic partner, "Less is more" is a powerful truism that applies not only to architecture but to interpersonal relationships as well. Fewer attempts at control result in greater harmony across the developmental spectrum for all of us.

CHAPTER 6

Luck or Chance Has Been Badly Underrated

HOW OFTEN HAVE we encountered the notion that we can be anything we want, that all we need to do is work hard, and if we keep plugging away, success will find us and carry us to the top of that mountain of good fortune?

If only we were more assertive, more creative, more organized, or had better communication skills, we could make it *big* in the worlds of business, friendship, and romantic love. Just a little more effort, and we will get there, wherever that is.

Books with promising titles such as *How to Win Friends and Influence People*,[26] *How to Succeed in Business Without Really Trying*,[27] and *The Guide to Getting It On*[28] have been

---

26 Dale Carnegie, *How to Win Friends and Influence People: The Only Book You Need to Lead You to Success*, New York: Simon & Schuster, (paperback), 1988.

27 Shepherd Mead, *How to Succeed in Business without Really Trying: The Dastard's Guide to Fame and Fortune*, New York: Simon & Schuster, 1952.

28 Paul Joannides, *The Guide to Getting It On: Unzipped*, Oregon, USA; Goofy Foot Press, 1996.

around for a long time. All such books sell the idea that success is just around the corner and that nothing is impossible. If we climb the highest mountain and swim the deepest river, we will find that pot of gold at the end of the rainbow.

While all these optimistic messages are uplifting and inspirational, they also carry the subliminal communication that lack of worldly success is our own fault. We haven't read the right books, used the most effective strategies, or tried hard enough; otherwise we would be at the top of our game; we would have reached that pinnacle—that Mount Everest—of our professional and personal life, if only we had done enough of what it takes.

The problem with most of the success strategies is that talent and hard work alone aren't enough to make it BIG. We need to be in the right place at the right time. We need to have friends who can help us along the way. We need the kind of personality that endears itself to the decision-makers in our sphere. As the Irish would say, we need a little bit of luck to get where we want to go.

GENETICS AND EARLY ENVIRONMENT

From the moment of our conception, we had to contend with many factors that we had no control over. We had no say about the kind of genes we inherited that determined our appearance, our intelligence for the most part, our talents, a few personality traits, and our overall health. Did we wind up short or tall, blue or dark-eyed, light or dark skinned, chubby or thin, musically or mathematically talented, athletic or studious, quiet or loud? Did we inherit a genetic disorder or come equipped with mainly positive DNA?

In addition, we had no control of the uterine environment

in which we began our journey as human beings. We had no say about our mother's health during pregnancy and whether she tried to safeguard her health and ours. Did she drink too much, smoke, or take pills for her nerves? Did she eat the right kind of food? Did we come into the world with every possible health and genetic advantage, just a few, or deficits galore? Our first habitat affected many aspects of our well-being, and here again, we had no control over the cards we were dealt.

While the poet William Blake may have been unduly pessimistic, he dramatically conveyed the different worlds into which we are born in one of his famous poems. In it he wrote that some of us are born to "misery and endless night," while others encounter only "sweet delight."[29]

With our birth we arrived into a specific family at a specific time and place. Was our arrival eagerly awaited or were we one of too many mouths to feed? How equipped was our family to deal with a new baby? Were they rich, middle-class, or poor? Well-connected socially or outcasts in their community? What ethnic group or clan did they belong to? How happy or depressed were our parents about their lives in general?

If our caretakers were stressed about our arrival or their work/family situation at the time, their anxiety affected us. Their anxiety impacted how consistently they attended to our needs and whether we were handled gently or roughly. Their worries affected our sense of security, communicating indirectly that the world is a safe place or an environment full of potential dangers. Their anxiety-driven behavior, which was entirely out of our control, profoundly affected our early days.

Our parents' personalities in general, over which we had no control, had a lasting effect. If our parents were impatient

---

29 William Blake, "Auguries of Innocence", *Poets of the English Language,* New York: Viking Press, 1950.

and irritable, they were conveying that we were more trouble than we were worth. Conversely, if they were consistently kind and accepting, they were communicating how important and worthwhile we were. Depending on their manner, we wound up feeling positive, negative, or somewhere in between about ourselves. In addition, our identification with a parent, usually the one we were closest to or the one with the most power in the family, shaped our own personalities for better or worse.

What was our birth order? Were we the firstborn in the family, likely to be intelligent and successful, or the more immature but carefree youngest child? Firstborns get the best and the worst of their parents' child-rearing attitudes and behavior. They get the most attention but also most of their parents' worries about being good parents. As a result, firstborns are most likely to internalize their parents' hopes and dreams of success, becoming achievement-oriented adults with a penchant for excessive concern about failure.

Middle children, on the other hand, have difficulty finding their unique place in the sun. While they might not have been ignored, they often do not have a special place in the family, and as a result are subtly hungry for attention. School infractions and minor behavior problems are common in this group.

In contrast to the "lost" middle child, "the baby of the family" gets lots of attention, but often for cute behavior that befits younger children. They therefore frequently have difficulty growing up and remain the charming but irresponsible child throughout adulthood.

PARENTAL EXPECTATIONS

Our parents' expectations of us profoundly affected how we turned out. Their wishes regarding our sex (did they want a boy or girl?), their hopes for our appearance (whom did they secretly wish we would resemble?), and their longings for specific talents in us colored our own satisfaction with who we are. If our parents were significantly disappointed with any aspect of our being, that disappointment could be internalized and become a source of self-criticism, even when the disapproval was totally unwarranted and irrational.

If we resembled the charming and successful uncle in our family, we were welcomed by the family with open arms. If, on the other hand, we looked or acted more like the loser relative who was forever in trouble with the law, our appearance and/or manner was probably a source of chagrin for our relatives.

The child who fulfills parental dreams and aspirations often becomes "the favorite child," while "the least-favored" represents parental fears and anxieties. In a musical family, for example, the child with musical talent might be especially cherished; in an athletic family, the muscular child with superb coordination might be the object of parental admiration. As for "the least-favored" status, it usually goes to the child who represents parental concerns about failure, aggression, or lack of social acceptance.

One beautiful, light-skinned African American woman who was a highly successful fashion model came into psychotherapy because her family hated the color of her skin, and by extension, she felt they hated her. As a result, she felt inferior to others, even though her accomplishments were extensive. Whether her family was envious of her good looks, rejected her for looking like an outsider in the family (they were all dark-skinned), or for some other reason was not clear, but their negative attitudes toward her were an ongoing source of pain and consternation for her. Until she was able to recognize that the dysfunction resided in them and not in her, her self-esteem took an unfair beating.

ELEMENTARY SCHOOL YEARS

Once we left the cocoon of our immediate family and ventured off into the world of school, we came into other important spheres of influence—teachers and peers. Typically, we had no control over which classrooms we were assigned, which teachers we got, and which classmates we sat next to. Whether we had nurturing and stimulating teachers and had wholesome peers around us or just the opposite was mainly the luck of the draw.

How were we influenced by our teachers? Besides their talent or lack thereof in inspiring us to love certain academic subjects, teachers affected our self-esteem in major ways. By their words or manner, did they convey that we were smart, average, or intellectually impaired? Did they, along with our classmates, communicate that we were likable or not? For many of us, being likable or lovable is at least as important as being smart.

No matter how well-adjusted teachers may be, they have their own unconscious biases and preferences. Most teachers prefer students who are the embodiment of their own values. As a result, well-behaved and verbal children receive most of the accolades in school and thus wind up with positive self-images intellectually, while the hyperactive and/or non-verbal children begin to see themselves as less intelligent and therefore less acceptable than their peers. No matter how beloved they were in their own families, the least-favored children in elementary school suffer from the years of being ignored or treated with disdain by their teachers.

While the adage "Birds of a feather flock together" has more than a grain of truth in it, many of the factors that affected our social development are outside of our control, and it is certainly true of our first friends. How were these early relationships formed, because of proximity, similarity, their initiative, or ours? Were these early friendships one-sided or mutual? What did we learn from them?

One woman recalled how her motivation to take care of others, established with a helpless, depressed mother, governed her early friendships. Feeling sorry for others propelled her into one-sided relationships where she was "the giver" and the other child "the taker." While these early friendships gave her a measure of satisfaction for being "a good child," they were far from growth-inducing experiences. It was only when she was in her forties that she discovered the gratifications inherent in mutual, reciprocal friendships. At that time she was living in a different part of the country, where she met several warm, compassionate women who were intellectually compatible. Their friendships, cemented by empathy and common interests, lasted a lifetime.

A young man named Tom recalled how his rejection by the boy next door when he was between five and ten years of age influenced his peer relationships for years. The neighbor boy, who was his age but much shorter, was sometimes warm to him and sometimes cold. One minute the neighbor boy was at Tom's house inviting him to play, and minutes later, he didn't want anything to do with Tom. While the neighbor boy was probably motivated by envy—both of his younger brother who was the family favorite and of Tom—his behavior was very confusing to Tom. More importantly, it resulted in Tom's internalizing the rejection and believing that there was something fundamentally wrong with him socially. It was only much later, in high school, when he discovered peers with mutual interests who appreciated his easygoing humor that he became more confident socially.

HIGH SCHOOL YEARS

Much has been written about the emotional upheavals of adolescence that affect all aspects of the fragile high school years. Fortunately for most of us, we survived that unstable time—the moodiness and the awkwardness, both physical and social, brought on by the overwhelming hormonal changes. Others were not as lucky. For them the scars from that period remained throughout life coloring their self-image as adults.

How traumatic were the teenage years for us? What did we do about the intense sexual feelings that were cascading through our awareness? Were we among the attractive, popular adolescents who breezed through this period or one of the dorky ones obsessed with our small size, large size, acne, or the many rejections that came our way? Whether we were unaffected by all the emotional upheavals of adolescence or deeply scarred by them was mostly a function of chance or fate and not our own doing. For the unlucky ones, feelings of inadequacy often persisted and affected professional and personal choices throughout the years.

During adolescence, serious mental health disorders, such as alcoholism, anorexia nervosa, depression, and schizophrenia, among others, can become apparent. Most of these syndromes are heavily influenced by genetics, but environment certainly plays a role. Here again, however, we are at the mercy of fate as to what kind of parents and childrearing practices we were exposed to. If we had angry, demeaning parents who repeatedly told us we were worthless, the negative effects of any genetic influence would be magnified. Conversely, if our parents were loving and compassionate, their positive impact attenuated negative genetic influences.

The interplay between genes, parental attitudes, and personal behavior is illustrated in the case of a chronic schizophrenic woman named Sally, who never recovered from her drug use during adolescence. Up until adolescence, she was a quiet, unassuming young girl, the youngest in a family of six, with very old-fashioned, strict parents. When she got into her late teenage years, she discovered boys and party drugs, which included LSD, and spent several years sexually acting out while on drugs. This combination of factors threw her into psychosis, later diagnosed as paranoid schizophrenia, a fate that debilitated her for the remainder of her years. She spent the rest of her long life, well into her seventies, in and out of mental health facilities and nursing homes.

In Sally's case, there was a family history of schizophrenia, so the genetic influence was easy to see. It was also apparent that her father was an angry, rigid man with a temper, and Sally's drug use during adolescence was clearly the final straw, the precipitating factor, that threw her over the edge. If she had not used drugs, would she have been saved, or was the schizophrenia ready to burst forth, no matter what she did? If she had a different father, would it have made a difference? Obviously there is no way of knowing, but her vulnerability as she entered adolescence coupled with her drug use doomed her to a life of tragedy and unhappiness.

COLLEGE YEARS AND EARLY ADULTHOOD

For those of us who made it safely through adolescence, we could not rest on our laurels and breathe easily as we headed into adulthood. Because we were still in the process of making the transition from childhood to adulthood, we could not count on smooth sailing from that point on. There were still many hurdles to overcome and decisions to make. What would we become professionally, and who would be our life partner? Would we have a family or go it alone?

If we went to college, the two major developmental tasks for this life period were making friends and choosing a major. Just as in high school, our friendships were affected primarily by proximity and similar interests. If drama was our love, then more likely than not our friends would be fellow thespians. The same is true for athletics, debate teams, or any other college pursuit. Or if we were in a sorority or fraternity house, our fellow Greeks would rank at the top of our friendship list.

As for choosing a major, again we were influenced not only by our own interests, but also by factors outside of our control—parents and friends who had their own ideas about how to succeed in life. While our parents may have wanted us to pursue medicine or law, professions we had no interest in, we may have loved academic subjects that they were not wild about. In such situations we had to decide whether to be "a good child" and follow their advice or go it alone and earn their disapproval.

For those of us who loved allegedly impractical subjects such as art, English, history, or music, we were especially conflicted about which major to choose. Should we follow the practical advice of our parents and pursue business, engineering, information technology, or science, the big money-makers, or follow our dreams and risk being poor and jobless? When the college deadline for choosing a major arrived, many of us were forced to pick a major hurriedly and haphazardly—one that led to a career we had to live with, for better or worse, through the years. For many of us those arbitrary decisions led to careers that we wound up being unsuited for and bored with.

Unknown to most of us during those years, there were and are ways of combining artistic dreams with entrepreneurial considerations. Interdisciplinary majors, such as managing the arts or music management, have been around a long time, and certain professions—law being a good example—do not require specific undergraduate majors. Unfortunately, most of us did not know the ins and outs of academia and how to make wise decisions about a major at that young time in our lives.

For first-generation college students, the first ones in their families to attend and/or complete college, these academic decisions are especially heart-wrenching. Because their families lacked experience and knowledge about how colleges work, these families were usually unable to provide their college-age children with accurate, prudent direction. As a result, first-generation students are often left to their own devices to figure out their professional pathways and are more likely to make unwise academic decisions. Then too, because money is such a survival issue in these families, poor academic decisions are costly, both to the student and the family. Changing career direction in college can impose a financial hardship on the family, because additional courses are usually required to complete a degree different from the one first chosen.

Maria, a first-generation college student born in the United States to a family originally from Honduras, wanted to be an elementary school teacher most of her life. However, her family had heard from friends and neighbors that teachers are paid poorly in the United States and that all good jobs go to engineers. With a great deal of pressure, the family convinced her to switch her major from education to engineering in her junior year, a decision that nearly wrecked her college career.

After Maria spent a semester in the College of Engineering, her grades plummeted. She had little aptitude for advanced mathematics and science, and she almost dropped out of college. Fortunately, with some helpful counseling, she was able to return to the College of Education, where she successfully completed her degree and began a teaching career that she continues to love.

MIDDLE AND LATE ADULTHOOD

Both our middle and later adult years were or will be influenced by luck or chance in significant ways. While we may have been well prepared for the jobs we applied for, whether we got them was a function of many factors outside of our control, such as our sex, ethnicity, personality, or references. For example, did we know somebody who had the boss's ear and could put in a good word for us? Was the boss especially enthralled by his alma mater and likely to give preferential treatment to graduates from that school? Did the boss really need a uniquely qualified person or an all-around worker at the time of the hire?

Hiring decisions are not always based on the person with the best qualifications, but on what the company is looking for. Based on the company's or department's current staffing, the human resources department may be trying to fill in personnel gaps. For example, the company may be missing a numbers person to handle finances or a good writer to help the organization obtain grants. Or the boss may be searching for a great salesperson who is funny and sociable rather than someone who is a marketing whiz. Or the person doing the hiring may be looking for an applicant who fits into the established culture of a department rather than a likely outsider. While some aspects of what a company is looking for are spelled out in its position postings, firms never list all the qualifications they are interested in. Thus, we really don't know which qualities will impress the managers involved in the hiring and on what basis they will make their final decision.

Sonia Sotomayor, the Supreme Court justice, wrote about her climb from poverty in the Bronx to her position on the highest court in the USA in her best-selling book, *My Beloved World*.[30] Growing up in a Puerto Rican family with an alcoholic father and a hardworking but distant mother, she attributed much of her optimism and success to the care and protection of her grandmother (*Abuelita*) but also acknowledged the role of luck or destiny. She wrote, "And that feeling of Abuelita's protection would only grow after her death, made manifest in countless ways, from bizarrely fortuitous interventions that would save my life in diabetic crises to strange alignments of circumstances that have favored me unreasonably. Things that might easily have happened to me somehow did not; things that were not likely to happen for me did. This seemed like luck with a purpose." In her biography what clearly emerges is that Sonia, while gifted and determined, was helped immeasurably by Puerto Rican groups throughout her career. In

---

30   Sonia Sotomayor, *My Beloved World,* New York: Vintage Books, 2013, 324.

addition, she was at the right place and the right time for her nomination and confirmation to the Supreme Court.

RIGHT PLACE AT THE RIGHT TIME

Being in the right place at the right time accounts for much of our good fortune, and the converse—being in the wrong place at the wrong time—is likewise true for our misfortunes. Timing is a dominant factor affecting much of our lives, and unfortunately it is a variable that we typically cannot manipulate for our own benefit. For example, we may be ready for a serious romantic relationship and fall hard for our work colleague, only to discover that he or she has just ended a disastrous romance and needs time to heal. On the other hand, falling in love with someone who is ready to fall in love with us will set bells ringing, for a while at least.

We may be a writer who just completed a novel, only to find out that a novel with a similar theme was published a few weeks earlier, so our manuscript gets rejected. Our timing was off through no fault of our own. Or we may be a chemist whose newly discovered compound fits the needs of the granting agency, so we wind up getting a grant to pursue its development. In the second case, the need for the product and its discovery coincided. While the different outcomes in the case of the novel and the chemical compound may have had little to do with the quality of the product, timing made all the difference in the success of the ventures.

No matter how much research we had done ahead of time, the success of each move we make in life is still a function of fate or chance. Because there is no way of knowing beforehand how well we will get along with our new peers or our new boss, for example, the luck of the draw will determine the outcome. Similarly, when moving to a new location, we have no knowledge of the neighbors and how congenial they will be. Whether we do well in buying or selling a house will depend primarily on the housing market at the time and not on our good taste or judgment. While the adaptability of our personalities has an impact on our adjustment to new situations, many aspects of a move, such as the people and tasks involved, are basically unpredictable factors requiring resiliency and creativity.

In addition, our final years are heavily influenced by physical health issues, which have a strong genetic component. Whether we will have heart or lung problems, arthritis, diabetes, or cancer will be influenced by genetics as well as our lifestyle. Then too, whether our health or mobility will be compromised by infections or accidents may be totally outside of our control.

While we do have control of our lifestyle choices, including our decisions about religion, friends, organizational commitments, exercise, diet, and alcohol or drug use, we have little say over our final moments. For most of us, when and how we die is beyond our control.

IN SUMMARY

Luck, chance, or fate, whatever we call it, has not been given the attention it deserves. As a result, our culture assigns too much personal responsibility to individuals themselves for how their lives have turned out. For those of us whose lives have been mainly positive, we wind up with an inflated sense of our own importance, and for those whose lives who have been marked by losses and tragedy, there is often excessive guilt and regret. Generally, we take too much credit for our successes and too much blame for our failures.

The United States is a country with entitlement and narcissism galore at the upper rungs of the social ladder, and at the lower end, many embittered, self-deprecating souls with little self-esteem. The widespread availability of social media enables us to measure our accomplishments regularly against those of our peers, and if we are doing better, we feel superior. If we are not doing as well, however, we wind up feeling deflated and inadequate. The reality that most high achievers come from high-status families with many social and economic advantages gets lost in our self-appraisals and judgments of others, and the opposite awareness—that many low achievers come from impoverished families with few resources—is likewise missing in our evaluations.

The best metaphor for life may be card games such as pinochle, poker or rummy, where the luck of the draw prevails. Just as we can't control which cards we're dealt in any legitimate card game, we have no control over the cards we're dealt in life, be it genes, parents, talents, health, or other factors. Regardless of the hand we get, however, we can play our cards to the best of our ability. Furthermore, we can learn to perfect our card-playing skills throughout life; that is, develop our talents and upgrade our limitations. If we manage to make the most of what fate has handed us, we can rejoice in our accomplishments, no matter how they stack up to those of our peers. While we cannot be anything we want, we can be the best self we were created to be. And that is quite an accomplishment!

CHAPTER 7

A Smidgen of Narcissism Adds Joy and Spice to Life

THE GOLDEN RULE, "Do unto others as you would have them do unto you," has been around for centuries. Dating back to early Confucian times (551-479 BC) at least, this concept appears prominently in Buddhism, Christianity, Hinduism, Judaism, and most world religions. The golden rule also appears in some form in almost every ethical tradition. "Treat others as you would like to be treated" is the message in a nutshell.

Frequent misunderstandings about this maxim occur, however, because we forget the word *as* in the directive. The golden rule does not state that we should treat others better than or instead of ourselves, but rather *as* we would like to be treated. The golden rule dramatically conveys the message that we are at least as important as others. If we try to follow this long-established commandment regarding human relations, we should give ourselves, in the form of attention, care, and credit, at least as much as we give to other people.

In this age of excessive self-concern and entitlement,

devoting too much attention to one's self can unfortunately sound like narcissism. Most of us don't want to be like the Greek mythological figure Narcissus, who falls in love with his own reflection. We don't want to be so filled with ourselves that we neglect others. We don't want to have a grandiose sense of self-importance that constantly craves attention. In short, we do not want to be boastful narcissistic personalities endlessly talking about ourselves, our accomplishments, and our important acquaintances whenever there is an opportunity. What, then, is unhealthy narcissism versus the healthy kind?

UNHEALTHY NARCISSISM

The characteristics of a narcissistic personality disorder are a pervasive pattern of grandiosity, excessive need for admiration, and a lack of empathy that begins in childhood or adolescence. Narcissists are the braggarts of the world, consistently overestimating their abilities and accomplishments and ready to tell others without hesitation about their real or imagined successes. Routinely comparing themselves to others, they believe they always outshine their peers. They see themselves as superior, special, and unique and expect others to see them the same way.

Narcissists also believe that they are entitled to special consideration, expecting favors or privileges from others, and when others are not forthcoming with compliments or gifts, they can become enraged. They also tend to be moody and manipulative, as well as charming, especially when trying to gain the attention and adoration they desire. Lacking empathy, they have only one view of the world: their own. They are closed off to other perspectives and filled with their own fantasies of success, power, brilliance, or beauty.

A CLASSICAL NARCISSIST

Sylvie, a sixty-five-year-old former actress, interrupted a psychology professor's lecture on existentialism with what she believed was a fitting segue. "Speaking of existentialism, acting is similar," she said, and then she launched into a lengthy and rambling account about her own experiences as an actress. Although a highly intelligent woman, Sylvie's narcissism clouded her judgment about what was appropriate in many interpersonal situations.

Conversations with Sylvie were markedly one-sided. When the other person was speaking about a topic she knew little about, she frequently changed the subject to a non sequitur by looking out the window and commenting on the outside shrubbery or the architectural wonders around her. She had inordinate difficulty in relating to topics introduced by others unless she happened to have a shared interest in the subject, which rarely occurred. Her conversations about herself, however, were lengthy, repetitious, boastful, and with little regard for the listener's time or interest.

While Sylvie read a great deal, she often used the shards of interpersonal wisdom gleaned from self-help books indiscriminately. For example, she misused the knowledge that people appreciate compliments by complimenting others in an effusive and often disingenuous manner. Her positive comments frequently fell on clearly unattractive items, such as an old, faded shirt or an unflattering haircut.

For all of us, whenever a compliment smacks of dishonesty, we don't know what to make of it and, as a result, we feel uncomfortable. Many of Sylvie's compliments appeared to be designed not to make others feel good, but to curry favor. Because she had an excessive need to be liked, her compliment- giving style served her well. Some people were flattered by her compliments and initially had a positive impression of her, but it faded quickly as they got to know her. Over time they found her to be a cold and pretentious woman.

Like many narcissists, Sylvie grew up in a poor family. As the oldest child in a family of eight, she had the major responsibility for the care of younger siblings—a role that earned her very little praise and attention in her family. Her parents were too busy to acknowledge her helpfulness and her younger brothers and sisters were resentful of her bossiness. In addition, her father, overwhelmed by all his family responsibilities, often behaved in a cruel, dictatorial manner with little patience for his children's playfulness. With Sylvie especially, he had little tolerance for her sassiness and/or demanding behavior.

As a result of the dynamics in her family, Sylvie identified with the upper-class families she read about or met in school. Her grandiose self, developed from these contacts, was a rigid set of dictates and rules about how to navigate the world. She valued hard work, stringent dieting, and glamorous apparel, while being disdainful of lower-class pursuits. For example, she wouldn't eat bread, potatoes, or stews—the staples of lower-and middle-class families in many countries—wouldn't watch television or go to the movies, and instead developed an obsession with ballet, classical music, highbrow reading, opera, theater, and travel. She pursued these sophisticated activities even when she could not afford them, and as a result was almost penniless in her retirement.

Sylvie's narcissism was unrelenting in its determination to spare her the experience of feeling inadequate; however, her feelings of inadequacy, while she was not conscious of them, were dramatically apparent when she was asked a question she could not answer. Rather than responding nonchalantly that she didn't know the answer, Sylvie would get visibly upset and respond angrily with something like, "How am I supposed to know something so unimportant?" She could not acknowledge mistakes or ordinary limitations like most of us, because any admission of ignorance or inadequacy jarred her sense of superiority. In Sylvie's case, her grandiosity hid strong feelings of inferiority.

NARCISSISTIC TRAITS

While Sylvie had a classical narcissistic personality, other people manifest narcissistic traits without having a full-blown, diagnosable disorder. Their narcissistic qualities, which may emerge only under stress, can be interwoven with positive personality features, such as agreeableness or conscientiousness. However, even when the narcissistic qualities of an occasional narcissist are not pronounced, these personality traits can cause considerable discomfort to others when on display. Chief among intermittent narcissistic characteristics is a sense of entitlement, demanding behavior, and inordinate concern about physical appearance.

Sense of Entitlement and Demanding Behavior

The sense of entitlement, which seems to be widespread in the twenty-first century, is an underlying belief that one has been especially endowed and therefore worthy of special consideration. The unique endowment may be the result of social class, rank, talent, accomplishment, money, or beauty, but whatever the distinguishing characteristic, it sets the person apart from the rank and file, opening the door to special privilege. Just as some nobility in old monarchies believed they were entitled to fame, fortune, and money as a result of their birthright, so entitled people today believe they should be treated in a similar fashion—as royalty—in a variety of venues.

The entitled among us believe they should not have to wait in long lines, should not have to be stuck in traffic, and should not be ignored in social gatherings. They should not have to share the limelight with others conversationally or on stage. They should be given the best seats in the theater, the best food at the table, and the most privileged position at the banquet. In short, the entitled feel deserving of the best that life has to offer, and when it doesn't occur, they become loudly demanding and insistent upon receiving their just due.

The people who push their way to the front of lines to catch a cab, take a picture, or get the best shopping bargains are all exhibiting narcissistic traits. The lessons from pre-school, kindergarten, and Sunday school about sharing toys or taking turns have long been forgotten and replaced by a me-first mentality. Hypersensitive to being ignored, the occa-sional narcissist reacts strongly to any perceived slight.

At a high school reunion, one elderly woman overreacted dramatically when she discovered there wasn't a printed name tag for her at the entrance. While the administrative mistake should have been easy to correct, the people in charge didn't bring along extra name tags, so the people staffing the tag table had no easy way to fix the error and quiet the outrage. Instead the error gave the narcissistic woman ample opportu-nity to play the role of the mistreated martyr, a role she ampli-fied with full-blown hysterics. For about an hour she greeted every newly arriving guest at the reunion with a dramatic ac-count of how humiliating her lack of a name tag was.

Narcissus and Narcissa

Besides a sense of entitlement accompanied by demanding behavior, inordinate concern about one's physical appearance is another narcissistic trait. During the first session of a psychotherapy evaluation, a woman who turned out to be the female equivalent of Narcissus was so positively taken with her reflection in the office window that she spent most of that session looking at her reflected self rather than making eye contact with the therapist. Although the preoccupation with her reflected image was by itself a diagnostic clue as to her narcissism, her failure to return for subsequent sessions prevented further validation of her personality. In general, narcissists have a hard time engaging in the reciprocity, mutuality, and self-reflection of psychotherapy and do not stay in therapy for any length of time.

Distinguishing run-of-the-mill pleasure in our physical appearance, or healthy narcissism, from the more pathological variety is not always easy. Preening before a date and enjoying our reflection in the mirror are part of grooming rituals that bespeak of healthy self-love. Whenever there is undue anxiety about how we look and an obsessiveness, such as spending hours worrying about our appearance, however, the high level of anxiety points to self-esteem problems. The exceptions are teenagers who are so beset by hormonal upheaval that they often worry inordinately about how they look. Their uncertainty about the attractiveness of their newly evolving, grown-up features creates anxiety, which is normal for this developmental phase.

With unhealthy narcissism, there is a fixation upon physical attractiveness as the defining characteristic of self-worth. For narcissistic men, having the physical body of Arnold

Schwarzenegger with gleaming muscles is well worth the exorbitant number of hours spent lifting weights. For narcissistic women, having the face and figure of a motion picture star is so important that it warrants inordinate effort in its pursuit. While some of this investment of time and money is beneficial to health and well-being, its excessiveness speaks loudly of its unhealthy origins. Too much energy, which could be used to enhance self-worth in other areas, is often used to cover up feelings of inadequacy. In addition, the success of these physical efforts is time limited, for ultimately the aging process wins out.

The unfortunate and unrelenting reality is that after twenty-five or thirty years of age, our bodies begin to decline. The physical accomplishments of early adulthood become harder and harder to maintain. Almost all professional dancers as well as baseball, football, soccer, and hockey players retire from their professional lives in their thirties or forties at the latest, because of the natural slowdown in prowess. For them and all of us who have invested a great deal of energy in our physical appearance, the aging process is psychologically difficult. The wrinkles are hard to erase with even the most expensive creams, and the sagging muscles are hard to keep firm with even strenuous workouts. It pays to have other talents and activities at hand as replacements for the diminishing ones.

Narcissistic Injuries

At times we get so wounded by an event or remark that it defies explanation, or a friend gets so upset by what we said or did that it leaves us baffled. We wonder why something so trivial, by any objective standard, could result in such a major upset.

One woman admitted to a psychiatric hospital with major depression reported that her downward spiral began after attending her nephew's wedding. When she arrived at the reception, she discovered that she was seated at a table some distance away from the bridal group, an assignment that left her feeling humiliated. She saw the table assignment as a demotion from her anticipated seat of prominence. She felt she deserved greater recognition on such an important occasion, but her assigned seating conveyed to everyone that she was not as important as she wanted to be. While she was not clamoring outwardly for special treatment that night, the degree of her upset conveyed her sense of entitlement that led to her hospitalization.

Whenever we overact to an insensitive or injurious comment, a degree of narcissism usually resides under the surface. We may feel wounded or hurt by another's behavior but lurking below those feelings is often a sense of entitlement. We believe we deserve to be perceived or treated differently. For example, we may see ourselves as kind and loving, and when a friend or relative tells us we are self-centered, we become outraged. "How dare he say something so mean when I am always so giving and generous to others?" we may think. When that happens, it is apparent that we have too much invested in the self-image of being a loving person and little awareness of other aspects of ourselves.

In a classroom discussion of anger, one narcissistic woman described herself as always loving and kind and said she never experienced anger. She remarked that anger was a total waste of time and didn't accomplish anything. The irony in her remarks was that her classmates saw her as one of the angriest women they had ever met because of the cruel and sarcastic comments she frequently made to others. Basically she was a rigid woman lacking self-awareness who manifested anger in her cutting remarks to others.

WHAT IS HEALTHY NARCISSISM?

Healthy narcissism can be found in the joy, delight, and/or pleasure we experience whenever we succeed at a valued activity. From our earliest days, healthy narcissism appears in the smiles or squeals of delight manifest whenever we accomplish something worthwhile, from recognizing our mother's face when we are six weeks old to finishing a delightful meal at any age. Reaching for and grabbing a toy, holding our own sippy cup, sitting up, walking, uttering meaningful sounds, crawling, and walking are just a few of the developmental tasks in early years that elicit delight and pleasure.

Later we add to this repertoire of successes when we develop language and large motor skills. Talking in full sentences, running, jumping, throwing balls, feeding ourselves, and putting on our own clothes continue the ongoing healthy enjoyment of our bodies and its emerging skills. In the school-age years, we experience pleasure when we learn to read, do math, jump rope, ride a bicycle, or make a basket on the basketball court. Learning to sing, play a musical instrument, or dance, along with the acquisition of sports-related skills, are other accomplishments that typically elicit healthy narcissism. Healthy narcissism is emotional involvement with our self, a form of self-love that is nurturing and sustaining.

One depressed young woman who didn't experience much joy in life told her therapist that she recently saw an old family movie of herself when she was three years old in which she was laughing and hamming it up in front of the camera. While most people would have been amused by the happy antics of an earlier self, she found her behavior as a child "disgusting because of how self-centered I was at such an early age." Somewhere along the way the young woman's zest for life got snuffed out by the adults around her, and her interpretation of narcissism became highly distorted.

Healthy Narcissism in Adults

As adults, we experience healthy narcissism whenever we feel pleasure playing a good game of golf, preparing a sumptuous meal, painting a landscape, finishing a crossword puzzle, or fixing a leaking pipe. It can also be seen in spontaneous, playful activities of all kinds. Any accomplishment can be a source of joy, provided we value the activity and our efforts surrounding it.

Taking care of our minds and bodies and experiencing pleasure in the process are also part and parcel of healthy narcissism. Feeling good after a workout or a lengthy run can be an adrenaline rush that fuels positive feelings about ourselves and life in general. Taking pride in our appearance and enjoying the many pleasures our bodies provide are also manifestations of healthy narcissism.

In disasters, accidents, and catastrophes of all kinds, healthy narcissism is evident in the victims' determination to overcome any physical diminishment. For example, many amputees in the military and in civilian life experience a sense of pride in mastering the physical skills necessary to feed themselves, bathe, and/or walk with the aid of a prosthesis. Even though the loss of a limb is initially devastating and an assault on one's identity, self-image, and autonomy, the pleasure involved in overcoming some aspects of the loss is evident in the broad smiles of amputees when a particular physical goal has been attained, such as standing on one leg or walking a desired distance with a prosthetic device.

For the elderly whose lives have become devoid of pleasure because old established sources of enjoyment have vanished, the pursuit of new adventures becomes important. Their old activities are often harder to pursue because of physical limitations, and their old friends are literally dying off. Senior citizen groups where camaraderie and novel activities abound can become new arenas for joy and discovery. There, the elderly can find the shared laughter about failing body parts and frequent doctor visits comforting and validating. In such an atmosphere where they are not alone with their limitations, they can enjoy a new, shared reality with like individuals.

SELF-ESTEEM AND NARCISSISM: TWO SIDES OF THE COIN

Self-esteem and healthy narcissism are similar but not identical. They usually go together but not always. Self-esteem defines how we view ourselves and how much we value that identity. For example, we can see ourselves as a smart, competent person with worthwhile characteristics but have a hard time enjoying life. The emotional *joie de vivre*, or healthy narcissistic component, may be missing as a result of constitution or upbringing. While there are emotional aspects to both concepts, healthy narcissism is decidedly more emotional than cognitive, while the opposite is true for self-esteem. Healthy narcissism embellishes self-esteem with positive, emotional flavoring that provides some immunity against depression and other mental health ills.

Eric Berne in his classic book, *Games People Play*,[31] identified three components of personality: the Child, Adult, and Parent domains. Basically the Child is the spontaneous, playful, and id-loving part of our personalities wherein healthy narcissism tends to reside. In contrast, the Adult is the more rational, logical, and problem-solving part, while the Parent contains the rules, prohibitions, and regulations for adaptive living. In Berne's model, self-esteem is more likely to be found in the Adult and Parent components, while healthy narcissism is clearly part of the basic biological self, or the Child.

The major point in delineating these two related concepts is to emphasize that healthy versions of both are necessary for a joyful and productive life. Sometimes in our child-rearing practices, we overemphasize the achieving and productive side while neglecting the emotional component of development. And yet being silly, playful, and spontaneous some of the time is as necessary to happiness as personal and professional success. In addition, the emotional liveliness that narcissism provides is vital to our being a good lover as well as a good parent.

With romantic partners, playfulness adds sexual energy and excitement to the relationship. Without emotional spontaneity, sex can be routine and boring, no matter how many books on how to have great sex were consulted. With children, reading them bedtime stories with dramatic effect and playing make-believe games with exuberance go a long way, not only in providing enjoyment, but in strengthening parent-child bonds. Having fun with family members is essential in keeping emotional connections vibrant. Laughter—an activity that occurs more regularly with healthy narcissists

---

31   Eric Berne, *Games People Play,* New York: Grove Press, 1964.

than with intellectual giants—continues to be one of the main ingredients safeguarding us from emotional isolation and depression.

IN SUMMARY

Not all narcissism is unhealthy. As with many other qualities, there are positive and negative kinds. Unhealthy narcissism consists of a sense of entitlement, demanding behavior, and inordinate concern about physical appearance. With even more serious varieties, there is grandiosity, an excessive need for admiration, and lack of empathy. Grandiosity is the belief that one is especially talented, gifted, brilliant, handsome or beautiful, or chosen by God for a special mission. In real or imagined possession of one or more of these extraordinary attributes, grandiose people feel superior to others and are typically boastful about their talents.

While it is important to convey to our children that they are special and uniquely loved, it is harmful to communicate that they are better than others and that they need to be *the best* in order to have value. This competitive mentality—always striving to be at the top of the heap—feeds into unhealthy narcissism. In addition, the grandiose need to be number one can be demoralizing when someone more talented arrives on the scene and takes over that cherished spot. The higher rates of suicide at more prestigious universities, compared to colleges having lower status, attest to the unhealthy aspects of the inordinate need to be number one no matter the personal cost to emotional and physical well-being.

In contrast to the unhealthy variety, healthy narcissism is a positive self-love that is nurturing and sustaining. It consists of the joy, delight, or pleasure that is experienced whenever we achieve something worthwhile, from simple physical attainments to complex intellectual achievements. It is the loud *"Hooray"* shouted from the rooftops when fortune smiles on us. It is the kind of pleasure, the *joie de vivre*, that makes life worth living. It is an affirmation that we have inherent value as human beings and that it is good to be alive.

CHAPTER 8

Empathy and Healthy Religion Go Hand in Hand

AT FIRST GLANCE, empathy and religion appear to have little in common. Empathy focuses on our relationships with others while religion emphasizes our relationship with God. However, both empathy and "healthy religion"[32] (the kind that is inclusive, universal, loving, and focused on our common humanity) are other-centered rather than self-centered. They both provide a perspective that reinforces our place in the universe alongside, not ahead of nor in opposition to, but with others. Cooperation is emphasized in both, not competition. Both empathy and religion, either directly or implicitly, stress altruism and compassion toward others. As a result, they mitigate against the kind of self-centeredness that feeds into entitlement and narcissism.

---

32 Richard Rohr, *The Universal Christ: How a Forgotten Reality Can Change Everything We See, Hope for, and Believe*, New York: Convergent Press, 2019.

UNDERSTANDING EMPATHY

While most of us are familiar with the concept of empathy, a few words of review may clarify why empathy is such a positive attribute. Basically, empathy is the action or capacity of understanding, being aware of, being sensitive to, and vicariously experiencing the feelings, thoughts, and experiences of another. It is understanding where another person is coming from, in terms of ideas and feelings, and communicating that understanding in meaningful language. It involves paying attention, not only to the words of another, but also to their feelings, which may be expressed most clearly in nonverbal behavior.

Nonverbal Messages

Facial expression, tone of voice, inflections, and gestures are all important in communicating meaning. The phrase, "Sure, I love you" can be said many ways, each of which communicates something different. When said softly and tenderly, the phrase expresses love and affection; when said sarcastically, it communicates resentment or disingenuousness. Likewise, the phrase, "What are you doing?" can express either simple curiosity or outrage, depending on tone of voice and accented words. A curious, soft-spoken "What are you doing?" versus a loud, angry version, where the emphasis is on the word *are* or on the word *doing*, are as different as night and day in terms of emotional impact on the listener.

In listening to other people and trying to understand their experience, we can get confused. Frequently the confusion occurs because the words don't match the nonverbal cues. Contradictions between words and nonverbal cues are signs of conflict in the speaker and lead to mixed messages. When someone says, "I don't care" and looks angry while saying it, it is obvious that the speaker has feelings about what has transpired. An empathic listener might comment, "You say you don't care, but you look angry." Or when someone frowns while saying "I'm just fine," the frown contradicts the spoken word and leaves the listener perplexed. Very often the speakers are not aware of the contradiction, so with an empathic response from a friend, they are helped to a greater understanding of what they are experiencing.

LANGUAGE OF EMPATHY

To communicate with empathy, the language needs to be geared to the emotional and intellectual level of the other person. If a kindergartener is upset because a boy in her class scribbled all over her coloring book, an empathic teacher or parent would respond at the youngster's level to communicate understanding. Talking about justice in an erudite manner would not communicate empathy to the child, but speaking about her feelings—how bad she feels when a mean boy ruined her coloring book—most certainly would. For all of us emotional words are better at communicating understanding than more abstract language.

The language of empathy typically consists of everyday expressions, including slang, not intellectual concepts. For example, when someone is really enjoying an activity or just scored a win, an empathic response might be, "Looks like you're having a ball" or "Sounds like you won the jackpot." With negative events or disappointments, an empathic comment could be, "Feels like you got the rug pulled out from under you" or "It really hurts when you don't get what you worked so hard to achieve." These examples emphasize feelings, which should be the focus of empathy, not the details of what transpired.

WHY IS EMPATHY IMPORTANT?

Facilitates Relationships

Empathic listening, which is the most important relationship tool around, helps us connect emotionally to others and as a result, feel less isolated. We learn that others experience the same difficulties and failings we do, that they share the same vulnerabilities, that they enjoy the same pleasures, and that the paths to success are similar from one neighborhood to the next. We also learn how to deal with difficult situations and avoid life's pitfalls by the positive examples of others. Empathy helps us relate to others, no matter their background or age, and in the process we learn a great deal about human nature. From our healthy relationships, we also absorb important values, positive attitudes, and effective coping skills.

The process of empathic identification also enables us to understand the beliefs and feelings of people who are different from us. Whether the difference lies in skin color, cultural/national background, sexual/political/religious background, or socioeconomic level, the difference is immaterial to our understanding of another person as a human being. Once we really get to know someone who appears different from us, we typically discover the universal human characteristics that connect us. Besides direct interactions, we get to know others vicariously by our reading, and film or TV watching. Without such experiences, we are likely to characterize others by erroneous stereotypes and are more prone to racism, homophobia, xenophobia, misogyny, and other distortions.

UNIVERSAL NEED FOR UNDERSTANDING

We all want to be understood—a fundamental need evident in early development with the toddler's repeated attempts to articulate sounds and convey meaning. This need, which gets more sophisticated as our language matures, is manifest in people of all ages and cultures. The need for understanding is apparent in young lovers who spend untold hours huddled together in conversation about their lives and their dreams. It is evident in groups of men talking together while playing chess or darts in parks and saloons, as well as in groups of women sitting together in corporate dining rooms or sewing circles. The desire to be understood by others and emotionally connected to them as a result is basic to human nature.

The rudiments of empathy are evident even in very young children. On one occasion a little girl about three years of age, after falling and hurting her knee, said through her tears, "Just like you, Grams." Apparently she identified her own pain with that of her grandmother's, who had recently undergone knee replacements. Further evidence of empathy's early appearance in development can be found in the anguished looks on preschoolers' faces when a tiny friend is hurt. Or the fear and sadness on the face of a younger sibling when a brother or sister is punished.

THE BENEFITS OF EMPATHY

Both the receivers and the senders of empathy benefit enormously. The receivers feel understood and the senders feel helpful. We can be helpful by doing something worthwhile for another person or by letting something positive be done to us. As someone once said, "The best way to help another is to let him help you."

Whether we are giving directions to a stranger or listening to a friend, in general we feel good about ourselves when we are helpful to another person. Our best self is enlisted when we are giving another person our attention, advice, affection, or assistance. While it is not clear whether the desire to be helpful stems from praise received from parents and other authority figures for helpful behavior or if it has a more innate source, it is safe to say that empathy and helpful behavior are universally valued. Emotionally tuned-in people make valued friends and coworkers.

A popular rendition of empathy is the concept of emotional intelligence,[33] generally defined as the ability to identify and manage one's own emotions and tune into the emotional states of others. People high in the Emotional Intelligence Quotient (EQ) are highly sought after in the business world because of the positive correlations obtained between EQ and job performance. Besides business and human resources, high EQ types make sensitive, compassionate helpers and leaders in a variety of fields, such as counseling, medicine, social work, and teaching.

STRENGTHENS ALTRUISM

In general, empathy strengthens our humanity—our compassion, sympathy, and/or consideration of others. In our movie and TV watching, we tend to identify with victims of all kinds and experience empathically their anguish and distress. We identify with victims of rape or assault, parents who have lost children, wives grieving for their deceased husbands, and soldiers mourning the deaths of their fellow combatants. In all

---

33 Daniel Goleman, *Emotional Intelligence: Why It can Matter more than IQ,* New York: Bantam Books, 1995.

126

these instances we feel empathy for the lost, vanquished, bullied, abandoned, and/or tortured—a compassionate identification that unites us with others and motivates our charitable behavior toward them.

We also identify with and feel empathy for the winners in life, which motivates us to perform positive actions for such heroes. Our identification with victors also feeds our self-esteem, but the benefits are only temporary when the achievements are not our own. The boosts in self-esteem from identifying with winning sports figures, Olympic champions, and media stars typically vanish by the day's end, but at the time of the victory, we feel energized and uplifted. The raucous shouting of the winning side after a victory can shake the rafters of halls and arenas, but the reasons for the celebration often fade into oblivion soon after the celebratory drinks at the local bar.

SUPPORT GROUPS

Longer-lasting benefits of empathy can be found in support groups of all kinds. At a nearby rehabilitation facility in Chicago, for example, patients had to confront their own tragic losses—of losing a limb to infection, accident, impaired circulation, or diabetes—and try to heal physically as well as emotionally. Right after the amputations, the patients' depression was palpable, but after several weeks of attending sessions in the support group, hope resurfaced as patients began to focus on mastering their prostheses and getting on with their lives.

From the consensus of the group observers and the patients themselves, the most helpful aspects of the groups were the high levels of empathy and support the patients had for one another. The patients listened with care and compassion to one another, gaining hope from those who were hopeful and providing reassurance to those who were hopeless at the time. Patients who were further along in the grieving process became role models for those who had just begun the journey. Like support groups of all kinds—Alcoholics Anonymous being the most popular example—such groups are based on the premise that empathic people sharing similar experiences can heal one another.

THE ROLE OF HEALTHY RELIGION

In both empathy and religion, attention is focused mainly on other people. Whether we are trying to understand others or love them, the emphasis is mostly outside of ourselves. Because of that fact, empathy and healthy religion can both be regarded as antidotes to the excessive narcissism that runs rampant in current society.

The history of religion is not replete with shining examples of virtue, however. The cruelties that so-called religious people perpetuated in the past, such as the Spanish Inquisition, the Crusades, Bloody Mary's persecution of Protestants, the Salem Witch hunts, Hitler's atrocities, and the Islamic jihads, have turned many good people away from organized religion. In acknowledging such past, grievous behaviors, a contemporary Catholic writer, Richard Rohr, writes, " Frankly, a new humility is emerging in Christianity as we begin to recognize our many major mistakes in the past, especially our tragic treatment of indigenous people in almost all the nations Christians colonized, along with our silence about and full complicity with slavery, destructive consumerism, apartheid, white privilege, the devastation of the planet, homophobia, classism, and the Holocaust."[34] In contrast to such abominations,

---

34   Richard Rohr, *The Universal Christ* (see note 32), p.206.

healthy religion is not divisive, violent, or discriminatory but beneficial, unifying, altruistic, and caring.

Even with organized religion's checkered past, the positive effects of regular churchgoing have been documented regularly by sociologists. Among the findings are that regular churchgoers are happier, commit fewer crimes, are in better health, live longer, drop out of high school less frequently, make more money, and finish college more frequently than those who don't attend church at all.[35] In addition, religious participation appears to foster an authoritative but warm, active, and expressive style of parenting that results in better relationships with children.[36] The shared religious commitment between partners also strengthens family ties and partner intimacy. In these families, domestic violence is less likely to take place than in families where church attendance is infrequent, such as yearly or less.[37]

WHAT DOES RELIGIOUS PARTICIPATION PROVIDE?

Among its many benefits, healthy religion provides a unifying philosophy of life that provides meaning to daily existence and a set of principles to guide daily behavior. In a world where competition, materialism, and consumerism rule, healthy religion provides an alternate and basically positive worldview that is rich in faith, hope, and charity.

Healthy religion that believes in a loving and merciful

---

35 J. D. Vance, *Hillbilly Elegy: A Memoir of a Family and Culture in Crisis,* New York: HarperCollins, 2016.

36 Lisa D. Pearce and William G. Axinn, "The Impact of Family Religious Life on the Quality of Mother-Child Relations," *American Sociological Review* 63, 6, December 1998, 810-828.

37 Christopher G. Ellison, John P. Bartkowski, and Kristin L. Anderson, "Are There Religious Variations in Domestic Violence?" *Journal of Family Issues* 20, 1, January 1999, 87-113.

God provides consolation to the grieving and hope to the downtrodden. Such religion is a storehouse of coping strategies to deal with life's failures, losses, and disappointments. If we believe that God accompanies us when we are depressed and assists us in getting through difficult times, we feel less lonely and isolated. Believers tend to weather catastrophes and disasters with less psychological distress than nonbelievers, and in the process feel supported by their God.

DIGNIFIES HUMAN NATURE AND PROVIDES RULES FOR LIVING

Healthy religion also provides a compelling and attractive foundation that grants dignity to all people.[38] Because healthy religion asserts that we are created in the image of a loving God, we are innately bestowed with goodness and decency. In addition, by virtue of being human, we are esteemed, honored, and endowed with certain inalienable rights that should not be violated (see United States Constitution). In effect we are elevated by healthy religion, not constricted or diminished.

As for rules for daily living, the Ten Commandments, which deal with our obligations to God and fellow human beings, are the foundation of the Judeo-Christian tradition. Other religions have similar rules governing everyday existence. In the Ten Commandments, for example, we are commanded to honor our God and our parents and to abstain from murder, adultery, thievery, lying, and excessive envy of others. Without moral and/or ethical principles of some kind, the world would probably be a more chaotic place full of unbridled greed, lust, aggression, disrespect, dishonesty, and corruption, among other deadly sins.

---

38 Richard Rohr, *The Universal Christ* (see note 32).

THE VALUE OF PRAYER

Honoring God, keeping holy the Sabbath day through prayer, and other rituals are foremost among the requirements of most religions. The Muslim calls to prayer five times a day are powerful, daily reminders about man's relationship to God. Whether the prayers consist of adoration, penance, petition, or thanksgiving is immaterial, since it is the very act of praying—the uplifting of minds and hearts to a supreme being—that matters.

When we are feeling totally helpless, prayer gives us some measure of control, especially in cases of death and other extreme tragedies. Being able to say, "I will pray for you" or "My prayers are with you" to a grieving spouse or parent who has just lost a loved one provides consolation to both the speaker and the victim. Prayers communicate caring and solidarity with the aggrieved person, essentially saying, "I am with you in your sorrow and hope that you will heal quickly."

In the support groups for limb loss previously mentioned, the number-one response to the question, "What gives you hope?" was prayer. When confronted with immeasurable loss, prayer clearly provided the most consolation and hope for the future. Other popular responses to that question were family and/or friends. Even with their amputations, many patients were eagerly awaiting special family events, such as graduations and weddings.

OPPORTUNITY FOR SELF-REFLECTION

Healthy religion encourages self-examination, not obsessive self-blaming or self-denigration, but a realistic focus on strengths and shortcomings. By looking at our attitudes and behaviors through the lens of self-improvement, we have an opportunity to self-correct and gain control of habits that are self-defeating, such as overeating, gambling, and/or excessive alcohol or drug use. Most cognitive-behavioral therapeutic programs, for example, begin by encouraging clients to keep journals as to when, where, and how much the unhealthy behavior is engaged in. By journal keeping and enhancing self-awareness, the process of change is often begun.

Self-awareness is also the goal of most psychodynamic therapies that facilitate insight into motives, conflicts, and defenses as a means of strengthening a person's capacity for self-regulation. The underlying belief of these therapies is that by gaining insight into ourselves, we are in a better position to control the tendencies that get us into trouble. In a similar fashion, healthy religion encourages self-understanding in order to grow and develop our potential as human beings. Unless we realize our shortcomings and limitations, we will not have the opportunity to monitor and correct them.

The recent popularity of techniques such as meditation and mindfulness is clearly a sign that self-reflection is not a luxury but a necessity in our increasingly technological and fast-paced society. Self-awareness, or psychological mindedness, leads not only to greater self-control, but also to a deeper understanding of human nature and greater compassion toward others.

A REMINDER ABOUT OUR PLACE

Healthy religion also reinforces our place in the universe. In Mary Oliver's poem "Wild Geese," [39] she writes about the joyous, celebratory honking of geese, each announcing his

---

39   Mary Oliver, "Wild Geese," in *Owls and other Fantasies*, Boston, MA: Beacon Press, 2003, 1

place "in the family of things," as they prepare to fly south for the winter. Likewise, we have a place in the family of things, as participants in this complex, evolving world of ours. As we stand witness to the grandeur of creation, healthy religion reminds us to be humble—to stand in deference to the scope and magnificence of the world. Awe and gratitude flow from the awareness of our place in the universe.

Humility, a virtue currently in short supply but one reinforced by healthy religion, is a counterpoint to the grandiosity, arrogance, and sense of entitlement that abounds in modern times. Humility is not proud or haughty, nor does it engage in excessive breast beating or self-denigration. While unpretentious, humility is not lowly or insignificant; it is an awareness that we are important but not the center of the universe. No matter our status or accomplishments, fundamentally we are on par with every other person. Subject to the same needs and laws, we are all creatures struggling to be loved and valued in this world.

Pride, the antithesis of humility, is not a positive virtue from the perspective of most religions. The biblical phrase "Pride goes before destruction and a haughty spirit before a fall"[40] reminds us of the fall of Adam and Eve that led to their banishment from the Garden of Eden. This biblical saying and many others warn us of the dangers of arrogance, puffery, and self-aggrandizement. Not only are boastful people likely to fall, but they are also not well-liked. Because we are not omnipotent, not in control of all aspects of life, and basically imperfect, the braggarts of the world are regarded by most of us as pretentious people, figuratively filled with "hot air." They have forgotten their place in the world.

---

40   Proverbs 16:18

Tangible Benefits

In addition to the benefits just described, religious congregations also provide material and psychological assistance to the disenfranchised. For lonely people seeking to belong, hungry souls in need of housing or food, the unemployed in need of job training, and/or despondent individuals bereft of hope, religion-based communities are oases of care. All major religions have community religious centers that meet the needs of the marginalized in a multitude of ways. Providing food and shelter, GED tutoring, counseling, educational programs, money management information, job assistance, childcare, and medical care are among the many services they may offer. The clients are equally varied: pregnant teenagers, victims of domestic violence, prisoners, senior citizens, and the disabled represent some of the many recipients, to name just a few.

HELPING OTHERS: THE COMMON INGREDIENT

Both empathy and healthy religion emphasize altruism, the unselfish regard for or devotion to the welfare of others. They both require attentiveness to the needs of others. To listen carefully—the first requirement of empathy—we need to have this basic regard for others; otherwise, why should we pay attention to what others are saying? In our hurried, demanding world, we may ask, "Who has time to listen?"

No matter how busy and stressful our work-related life is though, requests for empathy and altruism will flow freely from the intimate people in our world: emotionally close coworkers, family members, friends, and/or romantic partners. Because they know and trust us, our intimate relations will let us know when and how they need our help and understanding.

With our small circle of friends and family, therefore, there will be ample opportunities to be empathic and helpful, and to maintain these intimate relationships, we need to have honed these skills. The high divorce rates worldwide clearly indicate that we have not mastered the art of empathy even at home, so more focus on empathic listening in the family and elsewhere needs to be a part of our educational offerings.

For many of us, however, it is not difficult to be loving to close friends and family. Even Mafia members managed to do so, essentially because their intimate relations were regarded as extensions of themselves. Even in noncriminal families, the child who gets the most empathy is often the one who most resembles a beloved parent or relative. When we see ourselves in another, it is much easier to be understanding than when another person is perceived as different.

What about the wider world of strangers? Why should we be empathic and helpful to everyone we encounter—the ones who do not resemble us at all? Essentially because they too are our brothers and sisters. They too are our neighbors. In the biblical story of the Good Samaritan, the one who stopped to help the victim of a robbery was a foreigner; nevertheless, the Good Samaritan saw the helpless stranger as "his neighbor" and acted compassionately.

Along with healthy religion of all kinds, many writers, philosophers, and politicians have stressed the importance of helping others. Ralph Waldo Emerson wrote, "The purpose of life is not to be happy. It is to be useful, to be honorable, to be compassionate, to have it make some difference that you have lived and lived well." In a similar vein, Leo Buscaglia said, "It's not enough to have lived. We should be determined to live for something. May I suggest that it be creating joy for others, sharing what we have for the betterment of person-kind, bringing hope to the lost and love to the lonely."

Likewise Winston Churchill wrote, "We make a living by what we get, we make a life by what we give, and Gandhi said—and Mother Teresa demonstrated by her example, "The best way to find yourself is to lose yourself in the service of others." Buddha agreed when he wrote, "Set your heart on doing good. Do it over and over again, and you will be filled with joy."

IN SUMMARY

Empathy and healthy religion do go hand in hand. For all of us—the religious and nonreligious— empathic listening and responding are means of connecting with others and relating to them in a sensitive and beneficial manner. Because all of us want to be understood and valued, an empathic response from another person, in even our darkest days, facilitates the healing process. When we are behaving altruistically, we feel good about ourselves. Donating money to charity, providing a destitute neighbor with groceries, rebuilding a neighbor's house devasted by a tornado, or donating a kidney to a total stranger are all acts of compassion. Such behavior promotes self-esteem enhancement that is deep and durable.

Currently when most religions, especially Christian de-nominations, are losing members, it is easy to lose sight of the many positive benefits of religion. When it is not divisive, punitive, violent, or sectarian, but rather universal and wel-coming, religion is a godsend that reminds us of our place in the world. In addition, a healthy religion provides a unifying philosophy of life that gives meaning to daily existence and a set of principles to guide behavior. It also dignifies human nature.

Besides prayers, consolation, and support, caring communities affiliated with Buddhist or Hindu temples, Christian churches, mosques, and synagogues supply tangible benefits, such as food, shelter, job training, and educational programs to those in need. Such centers of worship are also hubs of connection and purpose.

When we are helping others, we manifest our best selves—the high roads in our nature—that lead to the deepest satisfaction. The old saying, "Virtue is its own reward," has much merit. Similarly, it can be said that pursuing goodness is the surefire pathway to happiness. By extending ourselves for the sake of others, we enrich our own lives a hundredfold.